LEGENDS of FAITH

Early Church FATHERS

Marilyn Boyer

First printing: May 2025

Master Books, P.O. Box 726, Green Forest, AR 72638

Master Books® is a division of the New Leaf Publishing Group, LLC.

ISBN: 978-1-68344-400-8
ISBN: 978-1-61458-935-8 (digital)
Library of Congress Control Number: 2025934917

Cover: Diana Bogardus
Interior: Terry White

Please consider requesting that a copy of this volume be purchased by your local library system.

Printed in the United States of America

Please visit our website for other great titles:
www.masterbooks.com

For information regarding promotional opportunities, please contact the publicity department at pr@nlpg.com.

Master Books®
A Division of New Leaf Publishing Group
www.masterbooks.com

Table of Contents

Image Credits

We created the interior images using Shutterstock AI.

Wiki: page 78.

Master Books: page 131.

Maps: *Map Trek,* pages 11, 21, 31, 43, 55, 71, 83, 95, 109, and 123.

Introduction: Jesus, Paul, and John

Just before Jesus **ascended** to heaven, He explained to His disciples what He expected them to do. We now call His instruction "the Great Commission." Jesus said, "Go therefore and make disciples of all the nations, baptizing them in the name of the Father and of the Son and of the Holy Spirit, teaching them to observe all things that I have commanded you; and lo, I am with you always, even to the end of the age" (Matthew 28:19–20). He wanted them to take the gospel message to all people everywhere.

ascended: To rise up through the air

What is this precious gospel message? John 3:16 tells us, "For God so loved the world that He gave His only begotten Son, that whoever believes in Him should not perish but have eternal life."

Jesus never sinned, but God treated Him as if He were guilty of every sin committed by any person who would ever believe in His name. He died in our place, paying for our sin by His death on the Cross. Anyone who believes in His name is credited with His righteousness. Jesus bore our sins so we could bear His righteousness and be allowed to enter His holy heaven. We have the privilege to serve Him with our lives. As 2 Corinthians 5:21 tells us, "For He [God] made Him [Jesus] who knew no sin to be sin for us, that we might become the righteousness of God in Him." This was the message of life-giving good news that must be spread around the world to all people.

However, before He left them, Jesus also prepared the disciples for the reality that some people in the world would not want to hear the message. Jesus' disciples should expect **persecution**. "If they persecuted Me, they will also persecute you" (John 15:20b). "The time is coming that whoever kills you will think that he offers God service. And these things they will do to you because they have not known the Father nor Me. But these things I have told you, that when the time comes, you may remember that I told you of them" (John 16:2b–4). Jesus promised to send the Holy Spirit to help His disciples. Not everyone would face persecution, but some would, and Jesus wanted to prepare His followers for whatever they might face. Jesus promised that He would build His Church (a group of people who are saved, not a building), and nothing could prevent it (Matthew 16:18), despite times of great opposition.

persecution: Ill-treatment

Paul

Saul of Tarsus was a man who was persecuting believers and putting them into prison just because they believed in the gospel. God had other plans for him. Saul was on his way to the city of Damascus to imprison more believers when a light from heaven surrounded him. He heard a voice saying, "Saul, Saul, why are you persecuting Me?" (Acts 9:4b). He was blinded, and his friends led him to the nearby city. God told a man named Ananias to go to him and tell him the gospel message. The Lord explained to Ananias, "Go, for he is a chosen vessel of Mine to bear My name before **Gentiles**, kings, and the children of Israel. For I will show him how many things he must suffer for My name's sake" (Acts 9:15b–16). Saul was specially chosen by the Lord to carry the gospel message to people who lived beyond Jerusalem and the surrounding areas. As the Lord **commissioned** him, He told him, "I have set you as a light to the Gentiles, That you should be for salvation to the ends of the earth" (Acts 13:47b).

Gentiles: People who are not Jewish

commissioned: Set apart for special service

His name was changed to Paul. He became the great Apostle who wrote many letters that became part of our Bible.

Paul did indeed have to suffer much for the sake of the gospel. He tells us in 2 Corinthians 11 that, among other dangers, he was beaten with rods, stoned, shipwrecked three times, suffered hardships from travel, experienced dangers from robbers, and spent time in prison, often being hungry and cold — all for the sake of carrying the gospel to others. He tells us in Philippians 3 that though he had suffered the loss of all things, he counted that but **rubbish** so that he might gain Christ and be graciously given Christ's righteousness through faith. In this way, we see how Paul was a faithful servant entrusted with preserving and spreading the gospel.

rubbish: Garbage

John

Paul was acquainted with the disciples of Jesus Christ. One of those faithful disciples was the Apostle John, who loyally served by Jesus' side while He lived on earth. John recorded much truth for us in the Gospel of John; the epistles of 1 John, 2 John, and 3 John; and the Book of Revelation. John was one of Jesus' first disciples. He was a son of Zebedee, a Galilean fisherman. He was present for most of the events of Jesus' earthly ministry. He was there when Jesus spoke the Sermon on the Mount. He witnessed many instances of healing and many miracles, such as the feeding of the five thousand people with five loaves of bread and two fish. He was also present at the Last Supper, in the Garden of Gethsemane, and at Jesus' crucifixion. It was John that Jesus asked to care for His mother after He died.

He was known as "the disciple whom Jesus loved," as he tells us in John 21:20. John recorded many of the events in the Bible which give us so much insight about Jesus' life and character. John 20:30–31 tells us his purpose for writing this book: "And truly Jesus did many other signs in the presence of His disciples, which are not written in this book; but these are written that you may believe that Jesus is the Christ, the Son of God, and that believing you may have life in His name."

John, too, had to face persecution because he believed in the gospel. He was exiled to the island of Patmos, a remote Roman colony in the Aegean Sea where prisoners were sent for punishment. Revelation 1:9 states, "I, John, both your brother and companion in the tribulation … was on the island that is called Patmos for the word of God and for the testimony of Jesus Christ." Historians think he was there a little over a year during Domitian's reign as emperor of Rome. We don't know how the Apostle John died, but it was of natural causes. It is thought that he died around A.D. 98 or 99 in Ephesus. John, the youngest of the disciples, outlived them all. We do know that during his life, he discipled a man named Polycarp, and this will be the first story in our book.

1

Polycarp

Disciple of the Apostle John

150 100 50 B.C. 0 A.D. 50 A.D. 69 – 155 300

"Eighty-six years I have served Christ, and He never did me any wrong. How can I blaspheme my King who saved me?"

Smyrna (Modern İzmir, Turkey) – Polycarp was born in Smyrna, an important ancient city in Asia Minor.

Rome – He traveled to meet with Pope Anicetus around A.D. 155 to discuss differences in the date of Easter.

Ephesus – Tradition holds that Polycarp was a disciple of the Apostle John, who ministered here. This city was a major center of early Christianity and may have influenced Polycarp's theological training.

Philippi – Polycarp wrote a letter to the church here, encouraging them to remain steadfast in their faith. This epistle remains one of the most important writings from early church fathers.

Smyrna Stadium (İzmir, Turkey) – Polycarp was martyred in the stadium of Smyrna around A.D. 155. His martyrdom is one of the earliest recorded accounts of Christian faithfulness under persecution.

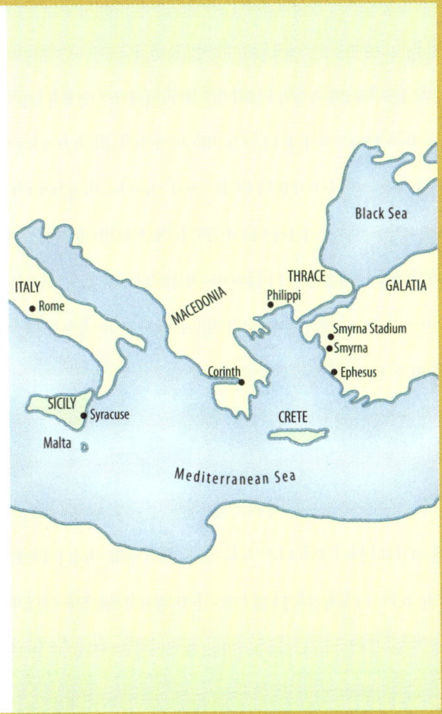

Who Was Polycarp?

Can you imagine what it would be like to learn about Jesus while sitting at the feet of the Apostle John? Well, that is exactly what happened to a man named Polycarp when he was young. When he was older, Polycarp became a **bishop** of Smyrna, in present-day Turkey. Polycarp became a **martyr**. He lived a long life. Roman authorities offered him the chance to save his life if he would deny Christ. He bravely responded, "Eighty-six years I have served Christ, and He never did me any wrong. How can I **blaspheme** my King who saved me?"[1]

bishop: An elder in charge of a local church or churches

martyr: One who dies for the sake of the gospel

blaspheme: Deny

Born to Christian Parents

Polycarp grew up in Smyrna, a large Roman province in Asia. His parents were Christians and taught him about Jesus. His grandfather had been a young man when Jesus died on the Cross and rose on the third day. One of Jesus' disciples, the Apostle John, had come to Smyrna. He told Polycarp's mother and father that Jesus had died to take the punishment

for their sins. He told them how Jesus had risen from the dead to offer them eternal life. Polycarp had opportunities to sit and listen as John related stories of how Jesus had healed the sick and made the blind see. John used to say, "All the libraries in the world could not hold the books I could write about Jesus."[2] Influenced greatly by John's teachings, Polycarp became a Christian at a young age.

History of Smyrna

Citizens of Smyrna were very loyal to the Roman government. The Romans worshiped many "gods" instead of the One true God. They became very concerned when Christians refused to worship other "**gods.**" Often when a disaster happened, the Roman people blamed Christians for angering the "gods." When the Christians refused to call the Roman emperor "Lord," Rome felt it was **justified** in persecuting the Christians.

> **"gods":** Statues, images, or even ideas worshiped instead of the One true God

> **justified:** Right

The Death of John

When Polycarp was about 30 years old, his friend Papias came with the news that the Apostle John was dying. Polycarp hurried to **Ephesus** to see his teacher one more time. However, because travel took so long, John passed away before Polycarp arrived. Polycarp remembered the words Paul had written in a letter to believers in Thessalonica: "But I do not want you to be ignorant, brethren, concerning those who have fallen asleep, lest you sorrow as others who have no hope" (1 Thessalonians 4:13–14). His friend reminded him that the Apostles had spread light to the world, but it was Jesus Christ who was the Light. It was up to Polycarp, Papias, and the Christians remaining on earth to pick up the torch of truth and pass it on to others.

Ephesus: A large city in Asia Minor

Bishop of Smyrna

Within a year of John's death, Polycarp was appointed bishop of the church at Smyrna. When the Apostle John was **exiled** to the island of Patmos, one of his letters was addressed to the church at Smyrna. It told the believers there they would be called to suffer.

At the end of the letter, he told them to be faithful unto death. He promised them a crown of

exiled: Forced to leave his country

life if they remained unwavering to the end. Polycarp taught this to believers and encouraged others to persevere no matter what might happen to them.

Christians not only had to deal with Rome's injustices, but some men began to spread false teachings. One group of these false teachers was called Nicolaitans. They were mentioned by the Apostle John in Revelation, where he condemned their practices. They were compromising God's truth and leading other Christians to take part in **pagan** religious **rituals**. Polycarp worked to teach Christians to stand steadfast, holding on to the truths of Scripture. He taught his congregation to "Be sober, be vigilant; because your adversary the devil walks about like a roaring lion, seeking whom he may devour" (1 Peter 5:8). He also taught his congregation to put off lying, anger, and bad language, and to put on love, kindness, forgiveness, and humility, as Paul wrote to members of the Galatian church.

pagan: Ungodly

rituals: Practices or ceremonies

Polycarp Is Hunted

In 155, several Christians were to be tried before the Roman **proconsul** in Smyrna during a pagan festival. A crowd of onlookers gathered to watch the proceedings. Three of the Christians gave in to the pressure to **renounce** Christ

proconsul: Governor of a province in ancient Rome

renounce: Formally abandon

when their lives were threatened by a tortuous death. One of the Christians, however, chose to cling to Christ and was martyred in a gruesome way. The crowd was wild and began hollering that they wanted to see Polycarp, the bishop of Smyrna, put to death. They reasoned that if the leader were killed, perhaps the Christians would just give up and worship the emperor.

Members of Polycarp's congregation helped him take refuge in an old, abandoned farmhouse. They were determined to protect their leader. They fixed him a nice breakfast, and after eating, Polycarp went to his room to read the Scriptures and pray for his people and for peace in Smyrna.

Sometime later, Polycarp joined his friends. They could tell something had upset him. He recalled being deep in prayer when he felt that he was about to be called to suffer a martyr's death. He was now 86 years old but still a very able man. His friends felt that they needed his guidance and leadership. He had been their beloved pastor for many years. They were shocked at his words but saw his deep resolve to be faithful to his Lord until the end.

Polycarp went to his room to reread a letter that Ignatius, an older fellow believer, had sent him many years ago, just before Ignatius had been martyred. It said, "Polycarp, a Christian is not lord of his own life, but he has time only for God. This is the work of God—and it will be yours too, when you fulfill your destiny. By grace, I trust that you are ready to do a good work for God. … Farewell in the Lord."[3] He held the letter to his chest while praying for strength and courage to meet his end. He also prayed that he would get an opportunity to share the glorious gospel with those who wanted to kill him.

Polycarp Returns Good for Evil

Search parties were looking all over for Polycarp. Suddenly, they burst into the farmhouse where he was staying. They demanded that Polycarp be turned over to them. Polycarp calmly greeted them, remarking that they looked tired and hungry. He invited them to sit and rest while his men prepared a fine supper for them. When the meal was ready, Polycarp asked for time to pray, and they permitted him. The Roman soldiers were amazed by his attention

to their needs. Polycarp sat in a corner of the room and, within their hearing, began to pray. The men heard every word as he prayed for them. No one had ever prayed for them before. He also prayed for the church at Smyrna, that his people would be faithful to offer the good news of the gospel to all men. After an hour, he joined the others for something to eat. It was late by then, and the **centurion** decided to wait until morning to transport him back to the city. The soldiers took turns watching Polycarp during the night, although Polycarp had no intention of escaping. He was ready to give his life for Jesus.

centurion: Roman commander

A Martyr's Death

It was February, A.D. 156, when the party reached the city gates of Smyrna. They were met by Herod, the commander of the Roman army, and Herod's father Nicetes. Herod asked Polycarp to climb into his carriage. He and his father questioned him as they entered the city. Polycarp answered them, pleading for Herod and his father to repent of their sins and call upon the Lord Jesus Christ for salvation. This angered Herod. He pressured Polycarp to say simply, "Caesar is Lord." As the carriage rode into the arena, Polycarp saw crowds of spectators waiting to see him put to death. In front of the crowds, he was told to proclaim allegiance to Emperor Antony. Calmly but boldly, Polycarp called out so all could hear, "Eighty-six years have I served Him [Jesus Christ] and He never did me any injury or proved Himself faithless. How then can I blaspheme my King and my Savior?"[4] Loudly, Polycarp proclaimed, "I am a Christian. I am a Christian." He was tied with ropes and burned at the stake while lifting his voice in prayer.

The Romans believed the way to defeat an enemy was to target and destroy its leadership. They had hoped to snuff out Christianity with this wicked act, but as Jesus promised, nothing could prevent Him from building His Church. Some of Polycarp's friends watched as he died. Later they wrote, "We will never be able to deny Jesus Christ. We will never be able to worship anyone else. We loved Polycarp and others like him. We will be disciples of the Lord Jesus Christ just like them."[5]

Shortly after Polycarp's death, the Smyrnaean church wrote a detailed account of his last days, as well as the words he spoke before he died. It was put into a letter and sent to the churches all over Asia Minor. What was meant to defeat the spread of God's glorious gospel was actually the fuel that lit a fire of inspiration and resolve in many believers. The Church of Jesus Christ grew more and more as a direct result of Polycarp's life and death.

2

Irenaeus of Lyon

Faithful to the Scriptures

A.D. 130–202

“*The world is at peace, and we walk on the highways without fear, and sail where we will.*”

Smyrna (Modern İzmir, Turkey) – Irenaeus was born in Smyrna around A.D. 130 and was a disciple of Polycarp, who greatly influenced his theological development.

Lugdunum (Modern Lyon, France) – He became the bishop of Lugdunum (Lyon) and played a crucial role in defending orthodox Christianity against Gnosticism. Irenaeus is traditionally believed to have died here around A.D. 202.

Rome – He traveled to Rome to appeal for unity in the church, particularly regarding disputes over the celebration of Easter.

Who Was Irenaeus?

Irenaeus (ee·ruh·NAY·uhs) was born around A.D. 130, about 100 years after Jesus Christ's death on the Cross. By the time Irenaeus was born, some people who called themselves Christians were spreading untruths. They claimed they had a secret they learned from Jesus that only special people could know. They called it "higher knowledge." They prided themselves on being more spiritual than other people. Their message was tempting to some, but many Christians were confused by this teaching. Irenaeus decided to write a book to help people understand the truth. His book is still useful today.

Student of Polycarp

Irenaeus was born near Smyrna, a large seaport town that attracted people from all over the world. He probably started school when he was seven. Usually, parents would join together and hire a tutor to teach their children to read, write, and do arithmetic. School began at dawn, and discipline was very strict. When children were 12 years old, they started studying classic writings of Greek and Roman authors, along with philosophy. Philosophy was the study of important questions

concerning the meaning of life. Irenaeus' writings show that he had read Greek poets and authors such as Plato and Homer.

He also had learned the Bible and the gospel message of Jesus Christ. Polycarp was his teacher and the head bishop in the church Irenaeus attended. You will remember that Polycarp's teacher was the Apostle John, who had lived and served Jesus during His time on earth. Polycarp instilled in Irenaeus the importance of being faithful to the teachings of Jesus Christ. Once, Irenaeus became so frustrated with men who were making up things, claiming that they were teachings of Jesus. He cried out, "O good God, for what times hast Thou reserved me, that I should endure these things?"[6]

In remembering Polycarp, Irenaeus said, "Whatsoever things he had heard from them [the Apostles] respecting the Lord, both with regard to His miracles and teaching, Polycarp having thus received information from the eyewitnesses of the Word of Life, would recount them all in harmony with the Scriptures. These things through God's mercy which was upon me, I then listened to attentively, and treasured them up not on paper, but in my heart; and I am continually, by God's grace, revolving these things accurately in my mind."[7]

Irenaeus was greatly grieved when his teacher Polycarp was killed. He was inspired by his faithful witness to the end of his life and was determined, like his teacher, to fight the good fight. In his mind, Irenaeus often pictured Polycarp sitting with his students. He remembered many things he had learned. His friends in the church in Smyrna could see how much Irenaeus wanted to serve Jesus. They believed God was preparing him to become a missionary and serve in a church in faraway France.

Eventually, Irenaeus moved to Lyon in France and became an elder in the church there. So, less than 150 years after Jesus died and rose again, Irenaeus was preaching the gospel to people in France. His congregation wrote that he was "zealous for the covenant of Christ."[8] Irenaeus loved to teach his congregation the message of the New Testament. He often explained the Gospels and writings of John to the people. People would come to him for help whenever there was confusion about whether certain teachings were true to Scripture.

Irenaeus Goes to Rome

The head bishop in Rome invited bishops from surrounding areas to come to Rome for a meeting. Here they would agree on what the Bible really taught. It was a journey of 330 miles, but Irenaeus was willing to go. In Rome, he met many Christian leaders. They were impressed by how well he understood and communicated the gospel. They encouraged his desire to write a book explaining the truth to others. He decided it was time to undertake the task. He had a unique way of teaching his congregation. He would preach the gospel of Jesus Christ, beginning in Genesis all the way through Revelation, the last book of the Bible.

Some false teachers called **Gnostics** taught that anything you could see or touch was bad. But Irenaeus taught the truth found in Genesis, that God made everything good. God created the world for His glory. He taught people that God made man and woman in His image. Genesis 1:31 says, "Then God saw everything that He had made, and indeed it was very good." Then Irenaeus taught them how sin entered the world when Adam and Eve chose to disobey God. Adam deserved to be

Gnostics: A group that believed in secret knowledge

punished for his sin. Irenaeus explained that since we are all members of their family, we **inherited** the sin nature, and our sin must also be punished. Then he would joyfully tell them the good news that the Apostle John had taught. God loved the world so much that He gave His only Son to take our punishment. Jesus did what we cannot do. He obeyed the Father, dying on the Cross in our place, and it is through His sacrifice that we are offered eternal life.

Irenaeus loved to teach about the "two Adams." Through disobedience, the first Adam separated us from God. Jesus, whom the Bible calls the second Adam, through His obedience, **reconciled** us to God. Irenaeus comforted the people by letting them know that one day, sin and suffering would be gone forever.

The parents in his congregation were excited that their children could understand Irenaeus' teachings. He had a gift for making things plain and clear. Even the children were dedicating their lives to the Lord Jesus. All were learning how to think properly when God's enemies did bad things to God's people.

reconciled: Restored

inherited: Born with

Writing Books

Irenaeus began writing a book to explain these truths to people. It took more than one book. He kept writing. Christians loved how clearly he explained biblical truth. He studied and researched to disprove the many false teachings that people were spreading. He used Bible verses for his proofs. He used humor together with reason to make his teachings more readily accepted. He continued teaching, preaching, and taking care of his congregation. In his spare time, he would write, sometimes far into the night.

He kept writing for many years, and when he finished, he had written five books. He entitled them *Against All False Teaching*. Today that series of books is called *Against Heresies*. A heresy is a teaching that someone claims to be biblical, but it goes against the teaching of the Word of God. He concluded, "Sadly if they [people] will not believe in the true God, and in the Savior Jesus, they will make up all kinds of things to believe."[9] He knew, as did the Apostles, that false teaching can keep people from going to heaven. Persecution, though, is only temporary pain to our bodies. Irenaeus' purpose in writing the books was to encourage Christians to hold fast to the biblical teachings of the Apostles. He included a prayer for the Gnostics. He claimed he loved them "better than they seem to love themselves."[10]

The Peacemaking Preacher

The name *Irenaeus* means "peacemaker." Irenaeus lived up to his name. During this time, the Roman government had political peace. This made it easier for people to travel safely to surrounding areas. Irenaeus used this opportunity to send missionaries all over the country of France. His teaching and preaching prepared men to do this. He encouraged his people to be grateful to the Roman government for the freedom Christians were enjoying at this time. He said, "The world is at peace, and we walk on the highways without fear, and sail where we will."[11] Although the Romans did not serve or fear God, Irenaeus understood that God appoints rulers "for the benefit of nations … so that under the fear of human rule, men may not eat each other up as fishes."[12]

This freedom allowed Irenaeus to preach and teach freely. A historian later commented that almost the whole city of Lyon had become Christian because of Irenaeus' preaching. During this time, the gospel spread throughout the entire region of France. Although things were peaceful, Irenaeus realized this was temporary, so he taught his people to be ready to die for their faith if necessary.

Persecution Comes

In A.D. 202, Septimius Severus became emperor of Rome, and persecution again raged against Christians. The last writing we have from Irenaeus is from A.D. 190. Historians believe he was killed for his faith in 202. Irenaeus is remembered best for teaching God's people to hold fast to the faith they received from Jesus and His Apostles. He trained them to defend the faith when others attacked it. Daily he taught others to read the Scriptures faithfully and humbly so they could distinguish historical facts from made-up stories. The gospel message remained pure. Jesus taught John, John taught Polycarp, and Polycarp taught Irenaeus. Through Irenaeus' writings, many have learned to guard the message of the gospel, some with their very lives.

3

Patrick of Ireland

From Slave to Missionary

A.D. 385–461

> *"It is not I but Christ the Lord who has ordered me to come and be with these people for the rest of my life."*

Bannavem Taburniae (possibly modern Wales or Scotland) – St. Patrick was born around A.D. 385, though the exact location is uncertain.

Ireland – As a teenager, he was kidnapped by Irish raiders and enslaved in Ireland for six years, during which he deepened his Christian faith before escaping back home.

Gaul (Modern France) – After escaping Ireland, he traveled to Gaul, where he trained in a monastery.

Downpatrick, Northern Ireland – Tradition holds that St. Patrick died around A.D. 461 and was buried in Downpatrick, where his grave is marked today.

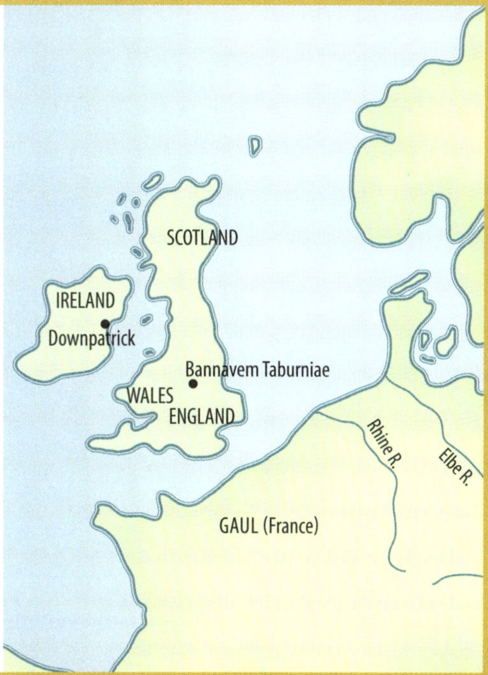

Who Was Patrick of Ireland?

Patrick of Ireland was born into a wealthy British family. His name was Maewyn Succat. When he became a bishop, he changed his name to Patrick, which means "father." As a teen, he was captured and forced to be a slave in Ireland. Here he found the Lord. He was able to escape back to his family and later became a missionary to the very country that had held him captive. It is through Patrick of Ireland that the legacy of the Early Church fathers was passed on to the Middle Ages. He carried the gospel of Jesus Christ to a new **era**.

era: A period of history

Early Years

Patrick was born around the end of the fourth century in a village on the western coast of Britain. Britain had been a part of the Roman Empire for 300 years. Patrick's father was a decurion, or city officer, in the Roman government. His father was also a **diaconum** in the church. His grandfather was the pastor. Even though Patrick was raised hearing the gospel, he later said, "I did not know the true God."[13]

diaconum: Deacon

Like most boys during that time, Patrick probably learned reading, writing, and arithmetic by studying under a **tutor**. It was customary for wealthy families to have slaves. These slaves did not belong to any certain race of people. Some had been captured in war, and some had sold themselves into slavery to pay their **debts**. Some had been **kidnapped** by men called slave traders, who sold men and women to make money. Patrick probably didn't have many chores, as the slaves his father owned would have done much of the work on their estate.

tutor: A person hired to teach children

debts: Money owed to others

kidnapped: Taken away by force

Kidnapped

One day, when Patrick was 16 years old, he was standing on a hill on his father's property overlooking the sea. Suddenly he saw several ships headed straight for his inlet. They appeared to be full of Irish **raiders**. Patrick began to run to his village to warn others of danger. The ships were approaching quickly. He must hurry. Running into the courtyard of his own home, he breathlessly called out to his father's servants, "Raiders from Ireland … they are coming now. We need to protect ourselves."[14]

raiders: Persons who attack and steal

He was too late. Strong arms grabbed him around the neck and swept him away along with many of the servants. Patrick tried to reason with them, telling them he was a Roman citizen, but the men wouldn't listen and probably didn't even understand his language. Patrick was taken aboard one of the ships and treated roughly. As the ship sailed away, he saw that his village was in

flames and many more people were being kidnapped. There was nothing they could do. There was no one to rescue them. When they arrived in Ireland, men and women were sold in the public square, just like his father had sold cattle. Patrick, the wealthy teenage boy, was now a slave.

Six Long Years

For six long years, Patrick was enslaved. The man who had purchased him placed him in charge of his sheep. Britain seemed so far away. To Patrick, the people seemed very **uncivilized**. Each morning, he would take the sheep out to pasture and protect them all day long from wolves and other wild animals. Each night, he brought them back to the sheepfold. He had to take particular care not to let any wander away. A slave who lost sheep was severely punished.

uncivilized: Considered wild and uneducated

Patrick had a lot of time during the day to think. He often wondered whether his parents knew what had happened to him. He felt so helpless and lonely. He began to wish he had paid more attention to the Bible when he had the chance in Britain. He realized he had ignored the one thing that could help him now in this difficult situation. Patrick developed an **urgency** to pray. He asked God to forgive him for never taking the Word of God seriously. He told God he had done wrong things for which he was sorry. He confessed that he didn't even know how to pray. He promised that if God would help him, he would do his best to serve Him. Patrick felt a great weight was lifted from him. At last, he didn't feel all alone. Patrick continued to feel a deep longing to pray. Sometimes he would pray as much as a hundred times each day. "I would rise to pray before dawn in snow and ice and rain. More and more the love of God increased and my sense of awe before God. Faith grew and my spirit was moved," he said.[15] He prayed so often that the Irish people started calling him "Holy Boy."

urgency: Strong need

During this time, Patrick was learning the language of Ireland. Most Irish people worshiped fierce gods and spent much of their lives in fear. A genuine concern for others grew in Patrick, something he had never felt before. "Before I was a slave, I didn't even care for myself," he later said.[16] As the weeks and months passed, he longed to see his family again.

A Long Journey

One night he had a dream which left him with a strong sense that God was telling him he would soon be going home. A few days later, he felt that a voice was telling him his ship was ready. He put together some provisions and gathered what little money he had saved. He left while the other slaves were still sleeping and set out in the dark and cold. There were dangers around him, such as wild animals and the possibility of being found and returned to his owner. "I went in God's strength, who was leading my life to a good end. And I feared nothing until I arrived at that ship."[17]

He would have to travel first to the west coast of Ireland and, from there, cross to the east shore, which was closest to his homeland. After traveling for weeks, Patrick arrived at a harbor on the western shore. There he saw a ship making ready to sail. A group of merchants was packing up goods for sale, along with a few dogs. Irish Wolfhounds were very valuable in those days. Patrick courageously asked the captain to take him along, but because he looked like a slave, the captain refused. Discouraged but fervently praying, Patrick turned to go. Suddenly, one of the sailors hollered to him that the captain had changed his mind. God had answered his plea.

Home at Last

The trip across the channel took three days. A storm arose, blowing the ship far off course, but finally, land was spotted. All went ashore, having no idea where they were. There were no towns, no people in sight. The men and the dogs trudged along for four weeks. Before long, they ran out of food. Patrick shared the gospel with the discouraged men. They begged him to pray for them and to pray for food. Amazingly, a herd of wild pigs came near them. The men quickly caught one, and soon the men and dogs had plenty to eat. The men began to treat Patrick and his God with great respect. Their needs were supplied each time Patrick would lead them in prayer. Eventually they came upon a village. The villagers were surprised to see a group of sailors so far from the sea.

The time had come for Patrick and the sailors to part company. Some of the sailors went in search of another ship on which to sail. Patrick set out in the direction that seemed to lead to his home.

He did odd jobs along the way to pay for food and travel expenses. Whenever he passed a church, he would stop and listen to sermons or Bible studies. He was so eager to soak up God's Word. Finally, his journey ended. It was a happy reunion when Patrick was reunited with his family! His father, in tears, told him he had thought Patrick to be dead. His mother was overjoyed and hoped he would never be away from home again.

A Call to Missions

A few years later, Patrick had another dream. This time in his dream he saw the Irish people saying, "Holy Boy, we beg you, come and walk among us again."[18] He recognized the voices as being those in the forest of Foclut, near the western sea where he had been a slave for six years. Never once had Patrick thought of going back to the land of his enslavement. He prayed to try to determine if this was just a random dream or if this was God's plan for his life. He hated the thought of leaving his family again. He finally concluded, "It is not I but Christ the Lord who has ordered me to come and be with these people for the rest of my life."[19]

He decided he needed to go to school first to learn Greek and **theology**. He began memorizing the Bible. He left to study theology in depth, probably somewhere in present-day France.

theology: The study of God

Home to Say Goodbye

Years later, he returned home, convinced he was finally ready to be a missionary to Ireland. "These last few years I've been preparing for the work that I know lies ahead. I have been getting to know the Bible and other Christian writings. I've been finding out more about prayer, worship, and self-discipline. I feel I am ready now to take the good news about Jesus to the people of Ireland," he explained to his aging parents.[20] His parents tried to convince him not to go, but in the end, his father took him to meet with the local bishop to get his blessing. After three meetings and more months passed, they finally made Patrick a bishop to Ireland. He would

now lead a group of missionaries carrying the blessed gospel message to Ireland. The new missions group gathered to pray before setting sail.

Ireland

At this time, there were no cities in Ireland, just scattered communities. Each community had a chief military leader in charge. Patrick's plan was to approach the chiefs of each community and ask permission to speak to their people. The first chief he met, whose name was Dichu, willingly invited him into his home so he could hear about this Jesus. He became a Christian — Patrick's first convert. He offered Patrick a barn to set up a church, the first Christian church in Ireland. From here, Patrick and his fellow missionaries planned their missionary journeys throughout the country. The message was not always accepted, however. At times, the missionaries were thrown in jail, robbed, and mistreated. Patrick was not discouraged. "If I be worthy, I am ready even to give up my life most willingly here and now for [Jesus'] name."[21] Patrick saw these hardships as opportunities to tell his captors about the love of Jesus Christ for their souls.

The Spread of the Gospel

Patrick and his band of missionaries traveled many miles, spreading the gospel to those who had never heard, and encouraging believers. Patrick was growing older. There were now many churches he had helped to establish throughout Ireland. The number of Christians now was too numerous to keep count. Speaking of the Irish people, Patrick said, "Such indeed is the case in Ireland, where they never had knowledge of God—and until now they celebrated only idols and unclean things. Yet, recently, what a change!"[22] Patrick would have loved to see his family again, but he felt compelled to preach the gospel to the Irish people. He set up communities where people could prepare to follow in his footsteps in the future. In years to come, these communities became models for Scotland and England. People traveled to Ireland to study from books Patrick had collected and instructors he had discipled. Less than 60 years after Patrick first went as a missionary to Ireland, thousands of Irish people had repented of sin and accepted the gospel.

Patrick Grows Old

As he became older and weaker, Patrick decided to write about his experiences of bringing the gospel to the Irish people. He said he was compelled to write because his gratitude to the Lord would not let him be silent. "I ought to shout out my thanks because God chose me for this task of bringing the love of Christ to the people of Ireland even though I was not wise or well-educated. I faced lots of dangers and problems in Ireland, and I was taken prisoner many times, but I could never have imagined, when I was young, just how much God would bless me in this place, with these people."[23] Of all the thousands of Christians now in Ireland, most had never even been to Britain. Patrick had truly done his part in extending God's Kingdom to the ends of the earth. Patrick had trained younger men to carry on the work he had begun. Patrick closed his writing of the story of his life by saying, "Anything I have achieved has been the gift of God. And this is my confession before I die."[24]

Patrick grew weaker and died on March 17, A.D. 493, the day many people now celebrate as St. Patrick's Day. Many Christians were inspired by his example to become missionaries, traveling all over Scotland, Europe, Britain, and even Germany. Followers of Patrick buried him in the land that Dichu had given him to build the first Christian church in Ireland. His friends remembered the date of his death. They passed it down from generation to generation, along with stories of what he had accomplished in Ireland. Patrick of Ireland will never be forgotten.

4

John Wycliffe

Bringing the Bible to the People

1324–1384

"To live and be silent is impossible for me. The guilt of such treason against the Lord of heaven is more to be dreaded than many deaths."

Hipswell, Yorkshire, England – Wycliffe was born around 1324 in Hipswell or the nearby village of Wycliffe-on-Tees in northern England.

Oxford, England – He studied and later taught at the University of Oxford, where he became a leading scholar, theologian, and critic of the medieval church.

London, England – Wycliffe was summoned to London multiple times to defend his teachings before church authorities and gained the support of some English nobility.

Lutterworth, England – He served as a parish priest in Lutterworth, where he continued his theological work, translated the Bible into English, and died in 1384.

Who Was John Wycliffe?

"John Wycliffe was born during a time of great spiritual darkness. He has been called the 'Morning Star of the Reformation' because God used him to shine rays of light into the spiritual darkness of England and much of Europe."[25] His work helped prepare the way for the Reformation, which would come almost two hundred years later.

John Is Saved

John Wycliffe (WICK·liff) was born around 1324 on a sheep farm in Yorkshire, England. He likely received his early education from the village priest. When he was 16, John left home to attend Oxford University. He had studied there for three years when the dreaded Black Death came to England. It was a terrible plague spread by fleas on infected rats. The rats came to England on ships arriving from Asia. The fleas would bite a person, causing an excruciatingly

painful sickness. Often the victim would die between two and six days after having been bitten. It spread like wildfire and was ultimately responsible for the death of one-third of Europe's population. Twenty-five million people died. At the time, John was a student at Merton College, a part of Oxford University. Oxford postponed classes until the plague ended.

John was deeply affected by the **devastation** caused by the plague. He turned to the Bible for comfort and hope, spending many hours reading the Word. He spent much time on his knees **repenting** from his sins and seeking direction from God for his life. John placed his trust in the Lord Jesus Christ and promised to serve Him all the days of his life. He was overwhelmed with the thought that so many people did not have the light of Scripture to guide and direct them. The only Bible available at the time was written in Latin, and only scholars and religious leaders had access to it. There were no copies of the Scripture in the English language.

devastation: Damage

repenting: Asking forgiveness for

The Bible Banned

One hundred years earlier, the Church of Rome had ruled that common people were not allowed to read the Scriptures. They had also made it illegal for anyone to translate the Scriptures into English. This ban was still in place at the time of John's **conversion**, and he was upset by this. The church leaders were profiting from the common people's ignorance. They told people they could buy pardon for their sins. They sold what they called **indulgences**. John read in the Bible that Jesus Christ had already died as payment for all sins committed. People only needed to repent and make Jesus Lord of their lives to receive forgiveness. A godly professor, who taught that God alone could save sinners by His grace, affirmed his belief.

conversion: When one becomes a Christian

indulgences: Pieces of parchment sold to people as payment for their sins

At this time in England, there were many **friars** who lived together in buildings called monasteries. They survived by begging for food while traveling around the country. John had grown up respecting these men, who had originally started these communities to spread

friars: Men devoted to religious groups within the Roman Church

the gospel in England. Over the years, however, many lost their original mission and focused on selling indulgences instead of teaching the Bible. Talking with a friend, John said, "These monks are a dangerous hindrance to the advance of God's kingdom here on earth. Look at them selling those wicked indulgences. They are keeping the poor people in the dark when they should be showing them the light of Christ, who takes away the sins of the world."[26] He also spoke out against the head of the Roman Church, who claimed to be the bridge between man and God. John declared that Jesus Christ was that bridge, not a man. John had a burning desire to shine the light of Christ into the darkness of the world. He knew, however, that before he could get people to listen to what he had to say, he must finish his education.

Continued Education

Having received his Bachelor of Arts degree from Oxford University, Wycliffe was now able to lecture there. John gained much pleasure from teaching. People began to admire his love for the Word of God and his desire to follow its teachings. He was soon elected as a Master of Balliol College, a part of Oxford University.

The friars' false teachings about indulgences were a burden to John. He spoke out against them and wrote a paper entitled, "Objections to the Friars." His speaking against the friars caused King Edward III of England to become his friend. The king was required to collect money from the people and send it to the church in Rome. When John said he should not have to do this anymore, the king was pleased and supported Wycliffe's teachings.

The friars traveled around the country, teaching wrong doctrines to the uninformed people. Wycliffe began debating them and continued to write, exposing their unbiblical practices. Wycliffe's position as a teacher gave him "the opportunity to teach the next generation of clergy at Oxford to place their trust, not in the declarations of the **Pope**, but in the Word of God."[27] Wycliffe's classes were always packed full, and his students greatly admired their teacher. He admonished his students to "proclaim the Gospel of Jesus Christ so that people can repent of their sin, believe on Him, and receive the gift of eternal life."[28]

Pope: Head of the Roman Church

Wycliffe Becomes a Pastor

In 1361, John Wycliffe was offered the opportunity to become the minister of a parish in Lutterworth. He accepted readily. He felt it was his obligation to preach the Word of God and **refute** any teachings that opposed the Scriptures. His duty was to protect his congregation. John missed his students, though, and after a couple of years, he turned the preaching over to another pastor. He went back to Oxford to study again. John received his Doctor of Divinity degree in 1372. Wycliffe taught that salvation is "by grace alone, through faith alone, in Christ alone."[29] This earned him the title of "Evangelical Doctor." He wrote many books and papers exposing untruths that were being taught.

> **refute:** Prove wrong

Summoned to Rome

The Roman Church was not pleased with the things Wycliffe was saying about their clergy. Fearing the people would believe him, they pronounced him to be a **heretic**. He was **summoned** to appear at St. Paul's Cathedral in London. A huge crowd gathered to watch the proceedings. The Roman clergy brought many false accusations against Wycliffe. They wanted to have him imprisoned or killed to stop him from preaching. The crowd was upset and wanted to see Wycliffe released. Wycliffe was released but warned to stop his preaching against the clergy. Again, in the same year, 1377, he was summoned a second time. Many people were present who believed Wycliffe's teachings. They were protesting, wanting to protect their teacher. Unexpectedly, a message came

> **heretic:** One whose beliefs oppose what the Church teaches

> **summoned:** Called

from the queen-mother. She forbade the meeting to continue, proclaiming that the charges against Wycliffe were false. She ruled that Wycliffe was not a heretic and he should go free.

Wycliffe Defends Parliament

At another time, Wycliffe was summoned to Parliament to help present the case that it was not right for the pope to collect taxes from England. In a document called "Bundle of Weeds," John advised Parliament that England should defend herself against the pope's unreasonable demands. The pope was using tax money to pay the French army, which was then fighting a war with England and killing English soldiers. Wycliffe proclaimed it was only right if the pope used the funds collected to feed and care for the poor. Wycliffe succeeded in uniting the nation to stand against the power of the Roman Church. He was now a national hero. No one had ever defended England against Rome before. The church leaders, however, were furious at him and plotted to stop his preaching. "No man on earth, not even the Pope himself, was going to stop the 'Evangelical Doctor' from proclaiming the gospel of Christ. With all his strength, John would keep on calling all people everywhere to repent and follow Christ."[30]

Wycliffe Is Sick

In 1379, Wycliffe became very sick and drew close to death. The Roman clergy came to visit him. They begged him to take back all the things he had said about them. They told him that God would punish him by sending him to hell for all his heresy. In his weakened state, John lay listening to their words. Then he asked his friends to help him to sit up. He mustered the strength to look his accusers in the eye and boldly respond, "I shall not die, but live and declare the errors and sins of you wicked men more than ever!"[31] The friars, frightened by his bold courage, ran from the room.

The Bible in English

Wycliffe recovered and continued to speak out against the Church's ruling barring the common people from reading the Scriptures. He was determined to use whatever time he had left on earth to preach and teach the Word of God to whoever would listen. He wrote another book called *On the Truth of the Holy Scriptures*. He firmly believed that every Christian in England should have the right to read the Bible for themselves. He realized that he must begin to produce an English translation of the Bible. Until this time, the Bible had only been written in Latin. Copies were very expensive and only owned by a few rich people.

Oxford University, under pressure from the Roman Church because of his teachings, asked him to leave. Many of his students followed him to Lutterworth in England, where he had been pastoring previously. This group of men became known as John's

band of "Bible Men." Wycliffe and his helpers worked on translating the Bible from Latin into English. Imagine the **tedious** work of copying the Bible by hand! Finally, in 1380, the New Testament was completed.

tedious: Long and difficult

Wycliffe's friend Nicholas Hereford continued translating the Old Testament. It was completed three years after Wycliffe died, in 1388. "The holy Scriptures exercised a reviving influence over men's hearts; minds were enlightened; souls were converted."[32]

John continued training his group of Bible Men to carry the gospel message all over the country. They preached the gospel "in churchyards, at fairs, in marketplaces, in the streets, and wherever they could get people to come and hear them."[33] Wycliffe exhorted his men to clearly preach the gospel. "The preacher who preaches to the people without reading the Gospel and clearly explaining it to them, gives the people a meal without bread."[34]

Wycliffe Dies

Wycliffe had always wondered if he might be called to die a martyr's death. He was willing if God required that of him. He said, "To live and be silent is impossible for me. The guilt of such treason against the Lord of heaven is more to be dreaded than many deaths."[35] Wycliffe was not called to be a martyr, however. He lived to the age of 60. He had a stroke while preaching in his church at Lutterworth. It left him unable to speak, and he died two days later on December 31, 1384. His body was buried in the graveyard of his dear church at Lutterworth. Forty-four years later, the pope ordered that his bones be dug up, burned to ashes, and scattered into the Swift River. From the Swift River, his ashes then floated into the Avon River and then the Severn River. From the Severn, they flowed into the ocean. In like manner, the Word of God he preached made its way from Lutterworth, England, to the ends of the earth.

5

Martin Luther

Changing the World with the Gospel

1200 1250 1300 1350

1483 – 1546

“My conscience is captive to the Word of God. I cannot recant anything, for to go against conscience is neither right nor safe. Here I stand. I cannot do otherwise. God help me. Amen!”

Eisleben – Luther’s birthplace and the place where he died.

Mansfeld – Where Luther grew up after his family moved from Eisleben.

Erfurt – The city where he studied at the University of Erfurt and later joined the Augustinian Monastery in 1505.

Wittenberg – The most famous Luther site, where he taught at the University of Wittenberg, preached at the Town Church (Stadtkirche), and posted his *95 Theses* on the door of All Saints’ Church (Castle Church) in 1517.

Worms – Where he stood trial before Emperor Charles V at the Diet of Worms in 1521.

Augsburg – Where he met with Cardinal Cajetan in 1518 to defend his teachings.

Who Was Martin Luther?

Martin Luther came into the world during a dark time in Church history. The Christian Church no longer based its beliefs on the Bible only. It had invented new "doctrines" and adopted new practices that Jesus never taught. The leaders were misleading the common people. In his search to be right with God, Luther started a movement that came to be called the **Reformation**. He called the Church back to the purity of the gospel message. He is considered one of the most influential men in the history of Christianity.

Reformation: Period when the Church underwent a revival and returned to original doctrines found in the Scripture

Early Years

Martin Luther was born in 1483, nine years before Columbus sailed to America. He was born on November 10 in the small town of Eisleben, Germany. Shortly after Martin was born, his father Hans moved the family to Mansfeld to take a job working in the copper mines, where he soon became a **supervisor**. Martin was one of eight children. Early in life, Martin showed a **keen** desire to study and learn. His father planned to send him to school where he could study to become a lawyer. When he was 14, Martin finished his studies in the local school and was sent to study in nearby towns. School rules were harsh. Students were expected to speak Latin instead of German. This was the language of highly educated people in Europe. Students were expected to go door-to-door, singing to raise funds or receive food to support their schooling.

supervisor: Leader of employees

keen: Strong

Filled with Fear

In 1501, Martin entered the University of Erfurt and graduated in four years, with excellent grades. In his spare time, Martin loved playing the lute and singing with his fellow students. During the summer of 1505, he returned home for a long-overdue visit with his family. The area had just experienced a devastating sickness in which many people had died. This filled Martin with fear and thoughts of death. He was afraid he had not done enough to please God. He left to go back to college, planning to become a successful lawyer. However, God sent a storm that changed not only Martin's plans but Church history, too!

Martin was caught in a fierce thunderstorm. Terrified that he might die and find himself face-to-face with God, he cried out to St. Anne. He feared God, but St. Anne was a woman whom the Church declared a **saint**. In those days, people asked saints for help, and it was customary to promise something in return. He vowed to become a **monk**. He thought becoming a monk would be the best way to secure favor with God.

saint: Someone especially close to God

monk: A man who lives a secluded life in a monastery to spend time in prayer and meditation

Martin Becomes a Monk

In preparation for entering the monastery, Martin sold all his earthly possessions, including his musical instruments, his law books, and even his clothes. Monks only wore a tunic and cape. When he told his father and mother, they were extremely distressed. They had sacrificed in order to afford to send this son to school. Now, they thought, all that time and money had been wasted.

Luther entered the Augustinian monastery in Erfurt. He just wanted to find assurance that his sins were forgiven. He wanted to know he would go to heaven when he died. Martin strove diligently to be a good monk. He prayed extensively, worked hard, and studied constantly. The more he worked to keep God's commandments, however, the more he felt like a failure. He took his job too seriously. He often went without food and sleep to punish himself for his sin. He became so extreme that the other monks began to worry about him. One day, he even **collapsed** on the floor from hunger and lack of sleep. One of the older monks encouraged him to spend more time reading the Scriptures than fasting and punishing his body. One day while reading, he was drawn to a verse in Romans 1:17, "The just shall live by faith." He didn't know what this meant. He was still struggling to understand how to have peace with God.

collapsed: Fell

Luther Becomes a Priest

On May 2, 1507, Luther, age 23, was ordained a priest. One part of his job was to listen when people confessed their sins to him. He would decide what their punishment would be. Some punishments might be to recite a prayer a certain number of times, give a certain sum of money to the church, or fast without food for a certain number of days. He also went around visiting poor people and doing good.

In 1508, he was invited to become a professor at the University at Wittenberg. There he preached to monks, professors, students, and townspeople. He was liked and well-received. He was later asked to be a preacher in the town church. He accepted the position, but he still did not understand the saving grace of the gospel of Christ.

A Visit to Rome

In 1510, Martin was sent to Rome as a traveling companion to an elderly monk. Rome was known as the Holy City, and many people traveled there each year, hoping to earn God's forgiveness. Martin had the same hope. It was a long journey. He walked about 1,000 miles in two months. While there, he climbed a special stairway called "The Holy Steps." It had 28 marble steps, and people

were told to climb up the stairs on their knees to earn forgiveness for themselves or others. When Luther got about halfway up the stairs, he began questioning what he was doing. Those words from the Book of Romans came to his mind again: "The just shall live by faith." Climbing stairs on his knees could not be the answer!

In Rome, Martin was appalled at the **corruption** he witnessed that had crept into the Church. He saw leaders who cared more about **luxuries** than God. They were misleading people by encouraging them to buy indulgences, pieces of paper that supposedly shorten a dead person's time in purgatory. The Church was teaching that purgatory was a place people went after they died to be "purged" of their sins before they went to heaven. Purgatory was not a pleasant place to be, so people still alive were told they could purchase indulgences to shorten their relatives' stay in purgatory. There was a saying they used to encourage people to buy indulgences: "As soon as the coin in the coffer rings, the soul from purgatory springs!"[36] All over Germany, people rushed to purchase indulgences. Pope Leo X was having financial problems. He

corruption: Dishonest conduct

luxuries: Extravagant living

had been remodeling the Cathedral of St. Peter and still wanted millions of dollars to finish. The sale of indulgences helped pay for his project. Martin left the city with a different opinion than when he had entered. He was very burdened by what he had observed. Nowhere in Scripture could he find reference to either purgatory or the sale of indulgences.

Faith in Christ

Luther was back in Wittenberg by 1512. He studied to become a doctor of theology and began to teach again at the University of Wittenberg. He continued to pray and fast but still had no rest for his soul. He never felt that his sins were forgiven. Finally, that verse in Romans 1:17 came to his mind again: "The just shall live by faith." The Holy Spirit opened his eyes, and he at last realized that there was nothing he could do to save himself. Jesus Christ had done it all. He finally understood that God was not angry with him, but patient and loving. "In Christ's righteousness, God's wrath was satisfied, and sinners who believed in Christ by the grace of the Holy Spirit were saved. Luther was so overjoyed that he later wrote that he felt as if his soul went through the open gates of a heavenly paradise."[37] Martin Luther was a changed man! His life's mission now was to spread the good news of the gospel of Jesus Christ to people everywhere.

The Dawning of the Reformation

On October 31, 1517, Luther, **distraught** that the Church was leading people astray, wrote the ***Ninety-five Theses*** about purgatory, indulgences, and other false teachings. He then nailed them to the door of the Castle Church in Wittenberg. This one act is said to have started the Reformation, an act that changed the world! In a matter of weeks, all of Europe was talking about Luther's *Ninety-five Theses*. Luther had written the theses in Latin. They were soon translated into German and other languages. Many people agreed with Luther. The church leaders did not. Luther had hoped the church leaders would be glad to make changes and proclaim the truth, but they were not. While Martin was in Worms where he had appeared before the emperor, an officer was sent from the pope to demand that Luther **retract** what he had said.

distraught: Very upset

Ninety-five Theses: Points or ideas

Luther refused and told the officer to deliver the message that he had only kept the promise he made when he became a monk — to teach the Scriptures faithfully. The officer had been instructed to bring Luther back to Rome if he would not change his mind, but Luther had left by night and returned to Wittenberg.

A New Emperor

About this time, the German emperor died. Seven princes, including Frederick the Wise, the prince-elector of Saxony, prepared to elect a new ruler. Frederick liked Luther and promised to vote for Charles V as emperor of Germany only if Charles promised to protect Luther. Under Frederick's protection, Luther continued his preaching and studying the Word. He wrote a book called *To the Christian Nobility of the German Nation*, encouraging Church to change for the good. In another book, *On the Freedom of a Christian*, he wrote to explain his thoughts to Pope Leo peacefully. In response, Pope Leo gave Luther 60 days to repent, or he would **excommunicate** Luther from the Roman Church. Luther, convinced he was right about his interpretation of the Scriptures, burned the notice publicly by the city gate.

excommunicate: Officially exclude from the Church

The Diet of Worms

Diet *is pronounced as (DEET), and rhymes with sweet.*

Worms *is pronounced as (VORMS), with a long* o *sound.*

Luther was summoned to attend a meeting where he would be tried by German rulers. His friends begged him not to go. Before he left town, Luther wrote, "I know and am certain that our Lord Jesus Christ still lives and rules. Upon this knowledge and assurance, I rely, and therefore I will not fear ten thousand popes; for he who is with me is greater than he who is in the world."[38]

A diet was a council meeting where rulers of nations connected to the Roman Empire met to decide important political and religious issues. Charles V had promised Frederick the Wise that he would give Luther a fair trial. At the town of Worms, Germany, Luther was met by a crowd of 2,000 people cheering him on. The emperor demanded that he retract what he had said. Luther responded, "My conscience is captive to the Word of God. I cannot recant anything, for to go against conscience is neither right nor safe. Here I stand. I cannot do otherwise. God help me. Amen!"[39] Charles V and the church leaders then pronounced Luther an outlaw and authorized anyone who saw him to kill him. Charles V, however, did not touch him; he honored his promise to Frederick the Wise and let Luther depart.

Kidnapped

Frederick the Wise did not want to take any chances, so he arranged for friendly men to pretend to kidnap Luther in order to save his life. He was taken to Frederick's castle of Wartburg. When he arrived, he was met by an elderly man who said, "Good evening, my friend. Good evening and welcome to the castle of Wartburg. Your good and kind Elector Frederick has seen to all this. Wittenberg will be too dangerous for you, so he rather cleverly arranged your kidnap. Wartberg will be your home now, so let me show you to your rooms."[40]

Martin was now in hiding and would be for the next ten months. He used this time to compose Christian hymns, like "A Mighty Fortress Is Our God." He also worked to translate the New Testament from Greek into the German language. This was something he had desired to do for a long time. He wanted to give ordinary German people a copy of the Scriptures to read for themselves. In September 1522, the first edition of the German New Testament was published. Even though the pope had forbidden people from reading Luther's writings, 3,000 copies sold in just a few days. This edition sold out by December, and a second edition was needed. One of Luther's opponents wrote, "Shoemakers and women and every kind of unlearned person, whoever of them were Lutherans and had somehow learned German letters, read it most eagerly as the font of

all truth. And by reading and rereading it they committed it to memory and so carried the book around with them in their bosoms."[41] This is precisely what Luther wanted to happen. He completed the translation of the entire Bible in 1542.

Unrest in Wittenberg

While Luther was confined in Wartburg, there was unrest in Wittenberg. Some people who claimed to follow Luther began destroying images, artwork, altars, and other property of the Roman Church. Luther disapproved of this destruction. In March 1522, Luther returned to Wittenberg and preached. He told people that such destructive behavior was not honoring God and was against Scripture. Eventually, people listened, and the situation settled down but not until Roman armies killed 100,000 peasants, and much property had been destroyed.

Luther Finds a Wife

New inventions made printing faster and easier. Luther took advantage of this and wrote many books, essays, and letters, as well as hymns of the faith. He wrote more than 36 hymns. He also wrote special teachings to help pastors, teachers, parents, and children as they learned the Scriptures. Luther's writings influenced many changes in Europe. Many priests, monks, and nuns decided to leave the Roman Catholic Church. It was very risky for nuns to leave the convent. Under the cover of darkness, some nuns hid in empty fish barrels transported by wagons to Wittenberg. There, the women started new lives. It was there that Luther met Katherine von Bora, a former nun. Luther asked his father for advice about marrying Katherine. His father was thrilled with the prospect of his son marrying and starting a family. Martin and Katie, as he called her, were married in 1525. The event made news everywhere — a former monk marrying a former nun!

The couple lived a happy life and had six children. They remodeled an empty monastery, which they made their home. It had been given to them by John the Steadfast, a brother of Frederick the Wise. Visitors were always welcome. Several students boarded with them and joined in after-dinner discussions. The students busily wrote down tidbits of wisdom Luther shared. Their notes were later compiled in a book entitled *Luther's Table Talk*. After dinner, Martin would get out his lute and play music. Everyone would join in and sing. The Luther family was never wealthy, but they shared what they had with any visitor who stopped by. Katherine kept a large garden, which helped provide food for the family.

They also kept pigs, chickens, and milk cows. Katherine grew fruit trees. Martin delighted in spending time with his children and answering their endless questions. Martin and Katherine experienced deep loss when two of their daughters got sick and died, but they rested in the truth that they would see them again in heaven.

Martin Luther Dies

Early in 1546, Martin, aged 59, despite feeling old and weak, left home to go to Eisleben to help settle a dispute between two rulers over some land. On the way, he became ill; when he arrived, he suffered two heart attacks. His last one was on February 17. A friend asked him, "Are you ready to die trusting in your Lord Jesus Christ and to confess the doctrine which you have taught in his name?"[42] Weakly, Luther managed to answer, "Yes," and then took his final breath.

Martin Luther died in the city where he was born. His body was taken back to Wittenberg by wagon. Bells tolled in each village as the wagon passed. Luther was buried beneath the pulpit of Castle Church, where he had preached faithfully so many times. It was on the door of this same church 30 years previously that he posted the *Ninety-five Theses*. This was where the fire of the Reformation first started. John Calvin, another great reformer, wrote after Luther's death, "We regard him as a remarkable apostle of Christ, through whose work and ministry, most of all, the purity of the Gospel has been restored in our time."[43]

6

William Tyndale

The Bible Smuggler

A.D.1250 1300 1350 1400 ca. 1494–1536

"If God spares my life, I will make it so in England that the ploughboys will know more of the Bible than many of the priests do now."

North Nibley, Gloucestershire, England – Tyndale was born around 1494 in North Nibley, near Gloucester.

Oxford, England – He studied at Magdalen Hall (now part of Hertford College), where he gained a strong foundation in classical and biblical languages.

Cambridge, England – He continued his theological studies at Cambridge, where he was influenced by the Reformation ideas spreading from the Continent.

London, England – In 1523, he sought approval from church authorities to translate the Bible into English but was denied, leading him to flee England.

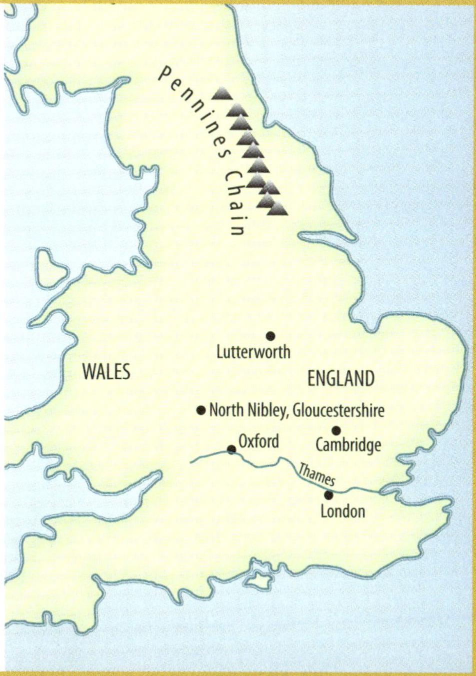

Who Was William Tyndale?

Sixteenth-century England was blanketed in spiritual darkness. The Bible was not available to the common man. Priests sometimes read from the Bible, but people could not understand them because they read it in Latin. William Tyndale had a burning desire to provide his countrymen with an English Bible so they could read it for themselves. He wanted to see a time come, as he explained, where the common farmer in the field would have a better knowledge of the Scriptures than the pope. However, the pope had forbidden anyone from translating the Bible. Therefore, Tyndale spent his life as a **fugitive** for the gospel of Christ.

fugitive: One who lives in hiding

Early Years

William Tyndale was born in the early 1490s in a small village in Gloucestershire, England. This was approximately 10 years after the birth of Martin Luther. William was born into a prosperous family of landowners, wool merchants, and farmers. Because his family was wealthy, he was able to attend Magdalen College, a part of Oxford University, at age 12. He studied at their grammar school before entering Oxford

University. He received his bachelor of arts and master of arts degrees at Oxford and then went to Cambridge University. Tyndale was ordained as a Roman Catholic priest in 1521. He was particularly skilled in languages. He could speak eight languages: Hebrew, Greek, Spanish, French, Latin, Italian, German, and English. Cambridge had been greatly influenced by Martin Luther's teachings. His writings were available to students, and Cambridge became the training ground for future reformers who tried to restore biblical truth to the Roman Church and its practices. It was here that Tyndale developed a deep commitment to the core truths of the new Protestant movement begun by Luther.

Tyndale Becomes a Christian

Men who wished to read or translate any part of the Bible in those days had to seek permission from the bishop. Very seldom was permission granted. Tyndale, however, was courageous and began to study the Scriptures on his own. As he read the Word of God more and more, the Holy Spirit began to work on his heart. He came to believe that the Bible was the infallible Word of God. He came to know and love the Lord Jesus, who became Lord of his life.

Tyndale joined a small band of students at Cambridge who met regularly to discuss this new theology. It had been just three years since Luther posted his *Ninety-five Theses* in Wittenberg, Germany. The students became known as "Little Germany." This little group became the **catalyst** for the English Reformation, which soon spread like wildfire across Britain. They told the other students that only the blood of Jesus could forgive their sins, not priests.

One day William was talking with a fellow priest. The priest commented, "I believe it would be better to be without God's law than to be without the pope's law."[44] To this remark, Tyndale cried, "I defy the pope and all his laws. If God spares my life, I will make it so in England that the ploughboys will know more of the Bible than many of the priests do now."[45]

catalyst: Spark

Tyndale Becomes a Tutor

About this time, Tyndale felt he needed to study the Greek New Testament more deeply. He left Cambridge, taking a job in Gloucestershire near his hometown as a tutor and private chaplain for John Walsh and his family. Walsh was one of Henry VIII's **knights** and quite a wealthy man. Each day Tyndale would tutor the Walsh children. He acted as chaplain for the family and functioned as a personal secretary to John Walsh. On Sundays, he preached at a small church in nearby St. Adeline. He spoke boldly, explaining the errors of the Roman Catholic Church against the truth of Scripture.

knights: Soldiers

He eventually realized that "It was impossible to establish the **lay** people in any truth, except the Scripture were laid before their eyes in the mother tongue."[46] In other words, he felt that a Bible translation in their own English language was desperately needed. The people needed to believe God, not William Tyndale. They must see truth from the Word of God. The church leaders were agitated by Tyndale's teachings, and it became clear to him that he needed to leave the Walsh home. He didn't want to cause them trouble. So, in the summer of 1523, he left.

lay: Common

A Bible for the People

Tyndale had a burning desire to translate the Bible into English. The English language had changed extensively since Wycliffe's translation. The Roman Church still forbade anyone to translate the Bible. Tyndale was terribly concerned with the fact that men and women were living and dying without true knowledge of the saving grace of Jesus Christ.

Tyndale found a sympathetic ear with a wealthy Christian named Humphrey Monmouth, who had heard his preaching. He offered Tyndale accommodations in his home while he worked on translating the Scriptures. While living there, Tyndale preached at St. Dunstan's Church in London. He drew crowds who came to hear the Word of God preached in a way they could understand. However, it was becoming increasingly dangerous in England for anyone who dared to merely read the Scriptures or anything written by any of the reformers. He was opposed by both the English Church and the crown. He sadly boarded a boat on the Thames River that was on its way to Hamburg, Germany.

Tyndale Heads for Germany

Monmouth had generously supplied Tyndale with money for his journey. He arrived in Germany in 1524. He left England when he was 30 years old and lived in exile for the rest of his life. For the next 12 years, he would remain an outlaw of the English crown. Never would he see his beloved homeland again.

William soon found someone willing to help him with the translation, a man named William Roy. It was too dangerous for Tyndale to stay in one place for long, so he moved to Cologne, Germany. He lodged in remote buildings, staying secluded as much as possible. He met Peter Quentell, a printer who used his press to publish the English New Testament. The printing press had been invented by Johannes Gutenberg in 1450. Without it, it would have been impossible to produce copies of the Bible fast enough to meet the growing demands of the people. The Reformation could never have spread as quickly as it did if the printing press hadn't been available.

In the summer of 1525, Peter Quentell began printing the first 22 chapters of Matthew. However, John Cochlaeus, an opponent of the Reformation, discovered that someone was translating the New Testament. He pretended to be a friend and uncovered the source of the printed Bibles. Soon Quentell's house was surrounded by soldiers, and the printing press was **seized**. Tyndale and Roy were warned shortly before the soldiers arrived. They barely had time to gather up some of the printed pages and flee to the city of Worms, where **Lutheranism** was flourishing.

seized: Taken by force

Lutheranism: Branch of Protestant Christianity based on Martin Luther's teaching

Tyndale Presses On

In Worms, Tyndale found another printer to help him carry on this work: Peter Schoeffer. Thousands of New Testaments were printed and ready to be distributed by the end of 1526. The copies looked different from Wycliffe's English version but were still quite distinct from what our Bibles look like today. The first printing produced 3,000 copies. Tyndale shipped his Bibles to England, hiding them in bales of cotton. Cloth merchants in England received the shipments, which were then secretly picked up by the Christian Brethren and distributed throughout England. Bibles were taken to many cities, universities, and even monasteries. It seemed as if all of England was eager for the Word of God. The Bibles were sold to merchants, students, tailors, bakers, weavers, bricklayers, and poor people. Each copy cost three shillings and two pence. This was equal to one week's wages for a skilled laborer and quite affordable for the average person.

Not everyone was happy about the Bible being distributed, however. The Roman Catholic Church passed a law forbidding anyone from buying or reading the Bible. They burned any Bibles they could find. Nevertheless, this did not stop the love of God's Word from spreading. Bishop Tunstall of London hired Augustine Packington, a merchant, to buy all the copies of the New Testament he could find. A huge bonfire was made near St. Paul's Cross in London, and the Bibles were burned. The bishop thought that would be the end of the books. Tyndale, however, took the money he received from the sale of the Bibles and printed more copies than before. Instead of stopping the circulation of Bibles, the bishop had helped it! "It seemed that for every Bible burned, many more Bibles appeared."[47]

More and more people helped to smuggle the Bibles into England. People's curiosity was **piqued**, and the sale of Bibles continued to increase. A man who sold Bibles in England was brought to trial and asked by the judge if he knew who was helping Tyndale print so many Bibles. He answered, "The bishop of London is doing more to help him than anyone else, for the money he paid to buy Bibles he ordered to be burned has been used to print new ones."[48] This is an example of how God used what man meant for evil to bring about good.

piqued: Excited or stirred

Tyndale Continues to Write

Tyndale continued to translate the Old Testament. He also wrote other books to teach Christian principles and responsibilities to the people. *Obedience of the Christian Man* explained what a Christian's duties were regarding the false claims of the Church during this time. Interestingly, Anne Boleyn, wife of Henry VIII, owned a copy of this

book and a copy of the Bible. She loved to read the Scriptures and books about them. She loaned a copy of *Obedience of the Christian Man* to one of her servants, who then loaned it to a friend. This man loved it so much that he dared to read it during a Catholic Mass. The book was seized from him and given to the cardinal. When the cardinal heard it belonged to the queen, he went to King Henry VIII. Upon discovering what had happened, Queen Anne went straight to the king. Bravely she said, "It is the dearest book that ever the dean of the cardinal took away."[49] She asked Henry to get it back for her and begged him to read it too. King Henry read it carefully, and although he never embraced the truth of the Word, he remarked to Anne, "This is a book for me and all kings to read."[50]

Tyndale is Captured

In 1529, Tyndale completed the translation of the **Pentateuch** of the Old Testament into English. He boarded a ship for Hamburg, intending to take it there for printing, but the vessel was shipwrecked off the coast of Holland. He finally ended up in Antwerp, where he had it printed in 1531, along with the Book of Jonah. Tyndale assumed he was safe in Antwerp and didn't bother to hide. He was wrong.

Pentateuch: First five books of the Bible

On May 21, 1535, Tyndale was arrested and imprisoned in the castle of Vilvoorden near Brussels. The prison was damp and dark, but his faith never dimmed. The other prisoners were encouraged by his cheerfulness and said, "If this man is not a good Christian, we don't know what is good anymore."[51]

Tyndale continued to translate while in prison. He wrote a letter to friends, asking for warm clothing and his Hebrew Bible to be brought to him. Roman priests visited him, attempting to convince him to return to the Roman Church. When they realized he never would, he was sentenced to death on August 12, 1536.

On October 6, 1536, 500 days after he was first imprisoned, Tyndale was brought to the castle courtyard. Here he was tried on a charge of heresy and condemned to death. Just before they killed him, he cried out, "Lord, open the king of England's eyes!"[52] He was executed, and after he died, his body was burned to ashes. He was 42 years old. Years earlier he had said, "Though they kill me, I will only gain a better resurrection."[53]

Something miraculous happened. The Lord answered William Tyndale's final prayer. Within a few years of Tyndale's death, King Henry made a law that a copy of Tyndale's Bible was to be placed in every church in England so that all the people could read it.

"The Bible is going to go forward in my country—in English."[54] A servant inquired why, reminding the king that he had spent so much time working against it. Henry told him to never mind about that — just obey his order. The Lord had changed King Henry's mind. A few years after Tyndale's death, this Bible was circulated throughout England with the king's blessing.

When the King James Version of the Bible was translated years later, Tyndale's translation was relied upon heavily. Estimates are that 75% of the King James Version is taken from Tyndale's translation. Now, almost 500 years later, we have many translations, but they are all based on Tyndale's original translation. William Tyndale's influence, because of his dedication and sacrifice, is still spreading to the ends of the earth.

7

John Calvin

Bearer of the Light

1250 1300 1350 1400 1450 1509–1564

"None of these things move me, neither count I my life dear unto myself, so that I might … testify the gospel of the grace of God."

Noyon, France – Calvin was born in 1509 in Noyon, a small town in northern France.

Paris, France – He studied at the University of Paris, where he was exposed to humanist and Reformation ideas.

Basel, Switzerland – After fleeing persecution in France, Calvin published the first edition of *Institutes of the Christian Religion* in Basel in 1536.

Geneva, Switzerland – He spent much of his life in Geneva, leading the city's Reformation efforts, organizing its church, and establishing his influence as a theologian.

Strasbourg, Germany – From 1538 to 1541, Calvin lived in Strasbourg, ministering to French refugees and marrying Idelette de Bure before returning to Geneva, Switzerland, where he died in 1564.

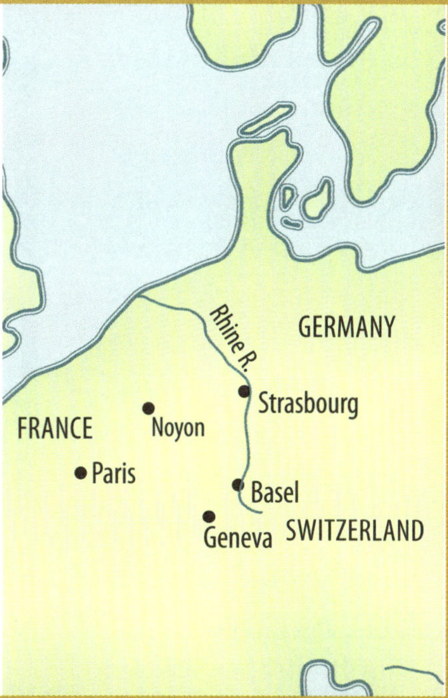

Who Was John Calvin?

John Calvin lived during a time when the Roman Church seemed to be more interested in money and power than being faithful to teach people the Word of God. The Reformation was the name given to a period in which some Christians struggled to return to the truth of God's Word. One of the most famous leaders of the Reformation was John Calvin.

Early Years

John Calvin was born in Noyon, France, on July 10, 1509. Noyon was a small farming community to the north of Paris. His mother died when he was only five years old, leaving his father to raise three young sons. His father worked as a lawyer for the bishop of Noyon. He made a good living and was able to hire a tutor for his sons' education. He soon recognized that John was exceptionally bright and made plans to send him to college when he became a teenager. He decided that his son should become a lawyer. At college, John learned strict personal discipline. He had to get up each morning at 4 o'clock to begin his day of classes. He learned to be diligent and productive, and those lessons remained with him throughout his life. Shortly after he obtained

a license to practice law, his father died. John decided to attend the University of Paris to continue his study of Greek and Hebrew, languages he especially enjoyed learning while in college.

Becoming a Reformer

In Paris, John was shown the writings of reformers such as Martin Luther. John was interested but very cautious. He had been raised to be a **devout** Roman Catholic, but he was curious because the Church seemed determined to keep people ignorant of the Bible. He learned that the Bible taught that man was saved by grace alone through faith alone. This was in opposition to the Roman Church's teaching that people had to earn their way to heaven by doing good works. Calvin claimed that it was God who helped him see that the Bible was the only source of truth when he was 24 years old. Through his private study, he was suddenly **converted**. He said, "God **subdued** me and made me teachable. Like a flash of light, I realized in what an **abyss** of errors, in what chaos I was."[55] Calvin concluded that the pope had taught people doctrine that was not true to Scripture. He felt he must become a Protestant.

devout: Deeply committed

converted: Embraced the gospel

subdued: Softened

abyss: Pit

Calvin on the Run

Soon after his conversion, the church authorities began persecuting Christians in France. Many had to flee, including John Calvin. He **disguised** himself as a farmer, carrying a hoe upon

disguised: Hid his identity

his shoulder, and left the city undetected. He spent a few months in different friends' homes in various French cities, including the home of the king's own sister, Marguerite d'Angouleme. She agreed with the Reformed theology. Everywhere he traveled, he secretly taught people the truth found in God's Word. A group of French Christians made lots of posters describing how the Roman Church was misleading people. On the evening of October 17, 1534, they hung them everywhere they could. There was even one hung in the king's bedroom! He was not pleased to find it when he woke up the next morning. More than 200 hundred people were arrested, and some of Calvin's friends were killed.

Calvin decided it was time to leave France. He and a friend left on horseback. They headed for Basel, a university town in Switzerland. Here he had peace and began to write a book called *Institutes of the Christian Religion*. In this book, he wrote a clear, concise explanation of what Reformed Christians believed and how these beliefs were based on Scripture. This became one of the most trusted books of the Reformation. He dedicated it to Francis I, hoping he might come to believe. This first edition was short, but he added to it throughout his life. He

started writing it when he was 26 and finally completed it when he was 50. People still use this book today.

More Travels

After this first edition was published, he headed to Italy, where he spent time as a guest of the **Duchess of Ferrara**. He finally decided to move to Strasbourg, a city bordered by France and Germany. On the way, however, he stopped at Geneva, a Swiss city on the border of France. Geneva was dealing with many problems. The people had just declared independence from both the government and the pope. The town was in disarray. The local preacher, William Farel, invited Calvin to stay and work with him in his ministry. Calvin was determined to go to Strasbourg to study in peace. Farel insisted he was needed in Geneva. Calvin said he felt like "God from heaven had laid His mighty hand" on him to keep him in Geneva.[56]

Duchess of Ferrara: An Italian noblewoman

Calvin in Geneva

Calvin worked hard, using skills he had learned in law school to help organize the struggling church. He wrote a catechism, which was a series of questions and answers used for instruction about God and the Church. This was done in order to make the Word of God clear and understandable to Christians.

Not everyone liked Calvin and his bold teachings. Some people even named their dogs after him to show their displeasure. Pope Pius IV, although he disagreed with Calvin, admired him. He once said, "The strength of that heretic consisted in this, that money never had the slightest charm for him. If I had such servants, my kingdom would extend from sea to sea."[57]

Calvin bore the scorn of the people, however, and declared, "None of these things move me, neither count I my life dear unto myself, so that I might … testify the gospel of the grace of God."[58] Two years later, both Calvin and Farel were given three days to leave Geneva, by order of the City Council. The people of Geneva had decided they did not want to listen to the reformers anymore. On April 23, 1538, both men left. Farel went to pastor in a nearby Swiss town.

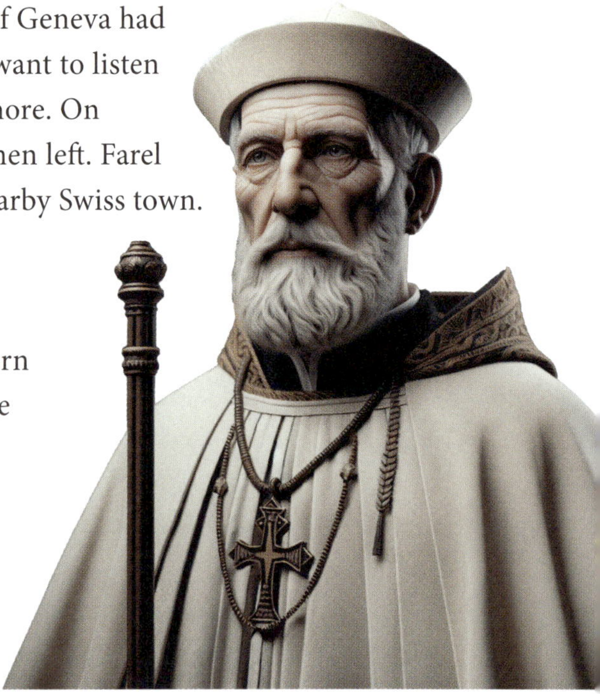

On to Strasbourg

Strasbourg, in Northern France, was now a free republic with its own government. It had become a **refuge** for

refuge: Safe place

many persecuted Christians. The people begged John Calvin to come be their pastor. Finally, he found rest and time to study. He loved pastoring in Strasbourg. He found time to write and added to *Institutes of the Christian Religion*. In this book, he taught that "The Bible directs Christians in all their living … we ought surely to seek from Scripture a rule for thinking and speaking. To this yardstick all thoughts of the mind and words of the mouth must be conformed."[59] He also wrote and published a psalm book and a commentary on the Book of Romans.

One night Calvin was invited to dinner at the home of Idelette de Bure, a widow with two children. He had visited her home when her husband was still alive and regularly conducted devotions with the family. Her husband had died from a plague that affected many people in the area. John continued to teach Idelette and her children. He found Idelette "upright and honest and even pretty."[60] John and Idelette were married in 1540. William Farel came to perform the marriage ceremony. With the help of his new wife, John was able to spend more time writing. He wrote simple commentaries so everyone could read and understand them.

Back to Geneva

In 1541, Calvin heard that things were not going well in Geneva. The Roman Church was trying to persuade the Protestants to come back. The Council of Geneva wrote letters begging Calvin to return and preach and teach in their city. He loved the congregation in Strasbourg and didn't want to leave them. It was difficult for Calvin to consider returning to the city that had banned him. He sought the Lord. He decided, "I am not my own. I offer up my heart as a sacrifice to the Lord. I submit my will and my affections to the obedience of God."[61] The people who had **banished** him were no longer in power, and now he was welcomed back with joy. In 1541, he returned. He was given a salary and a furnished house with a gorgeous view of Lake Geneva and the Alps to live in with his family. The Calvin house was often filled with guests, many of whom had escaped persecution in other countries. The Calvins welcomed them all.

banished: Gotten rid of

Much Work to Do

Calvin set about organizing the church with deacons, elders, pastors, and teachers, as taught in the New Testament. He preached two sermons

every Sunday and often during the week as well. He averaged preaching 200 sermons every year. He continued to write books to make the Word clear. He founded a college called Geneva Academy. It was one of the first Protestant colleges in the world. He trained hundreds of men from all over Europe who returned home, taking with them all they had learned, and they started churches. John Knox, a Scottish reformer, called the college "the most perfect school of Christ that ever was on earth since the days of the apostles."[62]

Family Tragedies

On July 28, 1542, a baby boy was born to the couple, but he lived only a few days. Calvin wrote to a friend, "The Lord has certainly afflicted a severe and bitter wound, in the death of our baby son, but He is himself a Father and knows best what is good for His children."[63] To another friend he said, "The Lord gave me a little son and then He took him away … In the kingdom of Christ, I have ten thousand children."[64] Sadly, Idelette died on March 29, 1549, after a long illness. Her death was very difficult for John. He confided to a friend, "I have lost the best companion of my life."[65]

Calvin Continues to Work

During his life, John Calvin wrote commentaries on almost every book in the Bible, in both the French and Latin languages. He produced three catechisms, many theological writings, and 4,271 letters to friends. He often counseled people who traveled long distances to seek his advice. People found him to be a gentle man who demonstrated genuine love for others and compassion for their trials. He often stopped to encourage a young boy walking down the street or write a note of sympathy if he heard that someone had experienced the death of a loved one.

As more Protestants heard about John Calvin, they fled to Geneva to escape persecution. Soon there were more Protestants in Geneva than Roman Catholics. He helped to get good laws passed that benefited people. Calvin established schools for young children. The Geneva Academy continued to train young men to become pastors who would spread the gospel. One of those young men was Theodore Beza, a Frenchman. He grew to be a dear friend to Calvin. He became a professor in the Academy, and Calvin trained him to carry on his work after he died. Beza saved all of Calvin's writings and later wrote a book about Calvin's life.

Calvin's Health Deteriorates

John had always suffered from poor health, but it was getting worse. He developed tuberculosis, which gave him bad chest pain and caused him to cough up blood. However, he continued to preach. Near the end of his life, he had high fevers and would wake up sweating during the night. Sometimes he was so weak that friends had to carry him to the pulpit in a special chair, but he was determined to live a life that glorified God! On days when he felt stronger, he took walks in his garden, but mostly he just worked. For years he had only eaten one meal a day. On days when he felt bad and had to stay in bed, he dictated words to his friend to write down. When friends suggested he just rest, he said, "What! Would you have the Lord find me idle?"[66]

On February 6, 1564, John Calvin preached his last sermon in St. Peter's Cathedral in Geneva. His cough became so persistent that he couldn't finish the sermon. From that time on, Beza preached, and friends carried Calvin in his special chair so he could listen. He wrote to his friend William Farel. "Don't get tired trying to come to me. I am already breathing with difficulty and expect every hour that my breath will stop completely."[67] Farel did arrive in time to say goodbye to his good friend. To pastoral friends who visited him, he said, "My faults have always displeased me … I pray you, forgive me the evil, and if there was any good, make it an example."[68]

He died peacefully on May 27, 1564, at the age of 54. He requested in his will that he did not want a gravestone to mark his burial spot. He said, "It is good that famous men should be buried in unmarked graves."[69] To this day, no one knows where his body was buried. However, on the 400th anniversary of his birth, the University of Geneva, which he founded, erected a statue of Calvin standing next to other great reformers such as William Farel, Theodore Beza, and John Knox. The city's motto is engraved under the statues: "After darkness, light."[70]

It has been said that John Calvin wrote what could be considered a fitting **epitaph** in his famous work *Institutes of the Christian Religion*: "We may patiently pass through this life in afflictions, hunger, cold, contempt, reproaches, and other disagreeable circumstances, content with this single assurance that our King will never desert us, but will give us what we need, until having finished our warfare, we shall be called to triumph."[71]

epitaph: Words written in memory of a person

8

John Knox

From Galley Slave to Fiery Preacher

A.D. 1250 1300 1350 1400 14

1514 – 1572

"*Although I am very weak right now, I am fully persuaded that I shall not die until my tongue shall glorify Him again in that same place.*"

Haddington, Scotland – Knox was born in this small town in East Lothian, Scotland around 1514.

St. Andrews, Scotland – He was influenced by Protestant reformers here and became involved in the movement. In 1547, he was captured and sent to the galleys as a prisoner.

Geneva, Switzerland – Knox spent time in Geneva, where he was deeply influenced by John Calvin's teachings and became a pastor (1554-1559).

Edinburgh, Scotland – He played a major role in the Scottish Reformation here. He died in Edinburgh on November 24, 1572, and was buried near St. Giles' Cathedral.

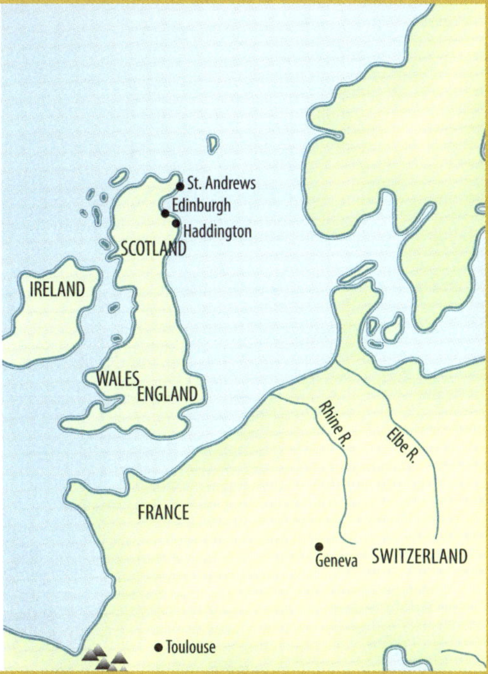

Who Was John Knox?

In 1514, Scotland was a small, sparsely settled country to the north of England that was greatly influenced by the Roman Church. Some Scottish people who had traveled to other countries had encountered some of the early reformers' teachings. One was Patrick Hamilton, who heard the gospel while in France. He spread the good news to Scotland, but authorities captured and killed him. The church authorities hoped this would stop others from adopting his beliefs, but instead, it was a fire that **kindled** the spread of the gospel. John Knox was 15 years old when Hamilton brought the gospel message to Scotland. He had no idea then that God would use him to become a powerful leader of the Protestant movement that would one day sweep throughout the country.

kindled: Started

Early Years

Not much is known about John's early life. He was born in Haddington, Scotland, around 1514; no one knows the exact date. As a young boy, he attended school near his home. He later moved to St. Andrews, Fife, Scotland, to attend the University of St. Andrews. Here he mastered debating and learned to speak with clarity and persuasion. God used this skill later in his life.

John Knox Becomes a Christian

John was raised in the Roman Church and was ordained as a priest in 1540. His job consisted mostly of checking documents for accuracy. Many things were changing in Scotland at the time. King James V had died, and the throne was left to his daughter Mary Stuart, who was only six days old. The Earl of Arran was chosen to make decisions for her until she grew up. Her mother, Mary of Guise, also acted as a **regent** for her after the earl.

Acting on behalf of the little queen, the earl decided to allow some freedom for people to read the Bible despite the Roman Church's disapproval. John Knox heard the message of salvation through faith alone preached in church, likely based on the Gospel of John, chapter 17. Knox later referred to this passage of Scripture as the point where he "cast his first anchor."[72] He became convinced that the Church was teaching things contrary to the Word of God. In 1543, he left the priesthood and joined the reformers.

regent: A person who governs a kingdom for a ruler who is a child

Becoming a Tutor

Knox was hired to be a tutor by two families. His students were three boys. He taught them Latin, English, and perhaps French. Both families were Protestants, so he taught them the Bible as well. For a time, Knox lived in peace, but soon King Henry of England sent an army to persecute the Scots. He even burned entire cities around the area where Knox was living. Scottish leaders looked to France for help, but the French were controlled by the Roman Church as well. Protestants were no longer free to openly proclaim the gospel.

George Wishart

Knox met and became good friends with George Wishart, a Protestant who had left Scotland because of the persecution. Wishart had traveled to Germany and Switzerland, where his faith was strengthened. Upon returning to Scotland, he began preaching passionately, both in churches and in the open air. A group of dedicated followers went with him. Knox became one of those followers, along with the two men who had hired him to tutor their sons. Knox and Wishart were

both about 30 years old. Although Wishart knew he would probably be put to death, he was determined to spread the truth of the Scriptures to anyone who dared to listen. Knox grew strong in the faith while being discipled by Wishart, and his convictions grew deeper. The Roman Church arrested Wishart on January 16, 1546, and condemned him to death. Knox determined to stay by his side, but Wishart told him, "Return to your pupils, and God bless you; one is sufficient for a sacrifice."[73] Wishart was killed on March 1. Knox was left as the leader of the Reformation in Scotland.

Knox Is Captured

Knox was persuaded by friends to live in a secluded castle in St. Andrews with fellow Protestants. Here he continued to teach students from April through July 1547. Daily, he taught the students the Gospel of John, explaining it thoroughly. A minister in a nearby church convinced Knox to help him preach the gospel. Knox didn't feel qualified, but the man finally persuaded him to take the position. In astonishing numbers, people came to hear the new preacher. Knox was known for his clear explanation of the Word of

God. He also was not afraid to explain how the Roman Church was misleading the people.

In those days, unrest was brewing between France and Scotland. It wasn't long until the French sailed to St. Andrews and captured the castle. Knox was taken captive with other Scottish Protestant men. They were forced to work as galley slaves. A galley was a long boat with sails, but when the wind subsided, it had to be propelled by oars. The men whom the French captured were forced to be slaves and were chained to their seats in the boat. They rowed for hours and were miserably treated. Many died from disease and overwork. Once a Frenchman handed Knox a picture of Mary the mother of Jesus and commanded him to pray to her. Knox refused and threw the picture into the river. He said the Scriptures taught that men must pray to God alone.

During a war, prisoners on a galley ship were forced to row very fast. Their diet consisted of biscuits and water with vegetable soup only three times a week. Many grew sickly, including John Knox. His fellow prisoners thought he was about to die. The man chained next to him tried to encourage him. He told him to look toward the land and focus on the church tower where he had preached his first sermon. Somehow Knox received strength to keep on living. He said, "I know it very well, for I see the steeple of the place where God first publicly opened my mouth to His glory. Although I am very weak right now, I am fully persuaded that I shall not die until my tongue shall glorify Him again in that same place."[74]

Winter came. Since the galleys could not sail, the prisoners spent their time making mats, blankets, and items to sell so they could use the money to buy extra food. Knox received a book from a friend who wanted him to revise it and divide it into chapters. He found much joy in this project. The book encouraged believers under persecution to go directly to God. It explained that salvation comes by grace alone, through faith in Christ alone.

Knox Is Released

Surprisingly, after 19 months of slavery, the French government freed the prisoners through a prisoner exchange agreement with England. This was at the beginning of 1549. Twelve-year-old Edward VI was now on the throne in England. Edward was a Protestant, and he was happy to have a fiery preacher like John Knox in his country. Edward's Royal Council sent Knox to Berwick, England, a small town located only three miles from the Scottish border. People in Berwick had not been exposed to the gospel, so Knox set about preaching. He also preached in nearby Newcastle. Many Scottish people crossed the border to come to hear him. Knox wrote another book while there to teach his people how to pray and how to trust God even during hard times. Here also, John Knox met Margery Bowes, who later became his wife. Margery and her mother loved to hear Knox preach the gospel.

Move to London

Knox was asked to move to London to become one of the king's preachers. He felt it was a good opportunity to spread the gospel. He corresponded with Margery and her mother during that time, answering many questions they had about how God could forgive their sins. He wrote, "Don't despair, Mother. God can forgive all your sins, even if you had committed thousands of them. What? Do you think God's goodness, mercy, and grace can be overcome by your iniquities? Will God, who cannot undo His work of salvation, be a liar, and lose His glory, because you are a sinner?"[75] This helped her realize that, of course, our sins are not greater than the grace Christ extends to us.

Trouble Again

King Edward died unexpectedly on July 6, 1553. His half-sister Mary Tudor (a daughter of King Henry VIII) became queen of England. She was Roman Catholic. She told Protestants they must either leave England or die for their faith. Knox decided to travel to France. He only stayed for a short time before leaving for Switzerland to visit two famous reformers — John Calvin in Geneva and Henry Bullinger in Zurich. He was so impressed with Geneva that he called it "the most perfect school of Christ that ever was on earth since the days of the apostles."[76]

Knox became a student of John Calvin and pastored a congregation of English people who had fled to Geneva to escape Mary Tudor. Calvin and Knox shared a friendship that lasted many years. In 1556, Knox and Margery were married. They enjoyed a happy marriage and had two sons, but sadly, Margery died after they had only been married for four years. Knox was heartbroken. Margery's mother came to care for the children and eventually took them to England to go to school. Although Knox was very happy in Geneva, he believed that God was calling him to return to his homeland to preach to the Scottish people. He knew he would have to live in constant danger there, but that did not stop him.

Return to Scotland

Knox returned to his homeland and immediately began to preach. One person commented that he was "able, in one hour, to put more life in us than five hundred trumpets continually blasting in our ears."[77] Knox preached the gospel fearlessly, pointing out the errors in the Roman Church. The queen ordered the persecution of Protestants, and it looked like war might be inevitable. However, this was avoided by the Duke of Argyle and the **prior** of St. Andrews, both of whom were friends of the reformers.

prior: One in authority of a religious house

Knox was planning to preach at St. Andrews again. He was warned that if he did, he would lose his life. Knox's friends begged him not to go, but he was determined. Even though soldiers were present while he spoke, he carried on, and God blessed his preaching. The Reformation spread, he did not lose his life, and he did preach again at St. Andrews, as he had determined he would while on the galley ship years before.

When Mary of Guise died, her daughter Mary Stuart became queen of Scotland. She was as wicked as her mother had been. On occasion, she called for John Knox to explain the Bible to her, and once, she was even in tears, but her heart did not change. He would end their meetings by praying that God would bless her and lead her to salvation. She was used to making those around her do whatever she wished. That didn't work with Knox. "Mary said she was more afraid of Knox and his prayers than an army of men."[78]

John Knox often spoke out against things the queen was doing. She finally had him tried for **treason**, but "Knox explained that he was not being disrespectful to her, but that he was being true to God, his country, and his conscience when he spoke against wrongs while promoting the right."[79]

treason: Disloyalty to one's country

Although many disagreed with Knox, his explanation was so clear and powerful that the queen and Church finally proclaimed his innocence. He was free to go.

Knox Continues Writing

In 1564, Knox married Margaret Stewart, and they had three daughters together. Margaret helped him with paperwork and was a wonderful wife. John Knox wrote several more books and tracts. In 1587, he wrote the *History of the Reformation in Scotland*. This is still one of the most respected books about church history. He also wrote books to help the Scottish Church establish its practices in accordance with Scripture.

John eventually returned to Edinburgh, a very dangerous place. Someone who knew he usually sat at his table with his back to the street shot a bullet through his window. **Providentially**, however, this day Knox had decided to sit at the side. The bullet flew over the empty chair on which he usually sat and hit a candlestick instead.

Providentially: Divine intervention by God

Knox continued to preach, although he was becoming weaker. A university student explained that Knox often had to be lifted up to the pulpit in order to preach. Once there, however, "he became so full of life that it looked like he wanted to beat the pulpit to pieces and fly out of it."[80]

Knox preached for the last time on November 9, 1572. He was in much pain but prayed, "To Thee, Lord, do I commit myself. Thou knowest how intense my pains are; but I do not complain. Yes, Lord, if such be Thy will concerning me, I could be content to bear these pains for many years yet, which in Thy just judgement Thou has laid upon me. Only do Thou continue to enlighten my mind through Christ Jesus."[81] On one of his last days, Knox asked his wife to read him his favorite chapter from the Bible, John 17, the very chapter that had led to his salvation so many years before.

God's faithful preacher died of **pneumonia** on November 24, 1572. At his funeral, the Earl of Morton,

pneumonia: Painful lung infection that makes it hard to breathe

a nobleman of Scotland, pointed in the direction of his coffin and said, "There lies a man who never feared the face of man. He has often been threatened with the sword, yet he ended his days in peace and honor, for God's providence watched over him in a special manner when his very life was sought."[82]

9

John Owen

Defending the Gospel with His Pen

"How is it that Jesus Christ is in Ireland only as a lion staining all His clothes with the blood of His enemies; and there is no one to show that He is a Lamb sprinkled with His own blood for His friends?"

Stadhampton, Oxfordshire, England – Owen was born in the village of Stadhampton, near Oxford in 1616.

Oxford, England – He attended Queen's College, Oxford, earning a B.A. (1632) and M.A. (1635).

London, England – Owen became a well-known preacher and theologian in London, serving as Dean of Christ Church, Oxford (1651-1660).

Coggeshall, Essex, England – He served as pastor at the Congregational church in Coggeshall from 1646 to 1651.

Ealing, London, England – Owen spent his last years writing theological works, and died on August 24, 1683.

Who Was John Owen?

John Owen was an English Puritan blessed by God with an intelligent mind, keen insight into God's Word, and the ability to express his thoughts clearly on paper. He was one of the most published writers of the seventeenth century. He believed the main goal of a Christian's life was to know God; he used his writing skills to point people to the Scriptures. He remained humble throughout his life. He never missed an opportunity to preach to countless people in the hope of leading them to a saving knowledge of Jesus Christ. Throughout his lifetime, he wrote more than 80 books, many of which are still read today.

Early Years

John Owen was born in Stadhampton, England, in 1616. He belonged to a group of people called Puritans. Puritans sought to worship God in a simple, pure way, following the example of

New Testament believers. John's father was a Puritan pastor who diligently taught the Bible to his children. John entered college at the age of 12. His rich uncle paid for his education with the intention that John would prepare for a good career with the Church of England.

While Owen was attending Oxford University, trouble was brewing in the British government. Parliament was not pleased with some decisions made by King Charles I. For example, the king invented new ways to tax the people to help support a war he started with Scotland. He was also beginning to punish Puritans because they did not teach and follow the ***Book of Common Prayer***. The Puritans felt this book was too similar to rules created by the pope and distracted people from true worship. Upon graduation, Owen realized he would have to accept many things he considered wrong if he wanted to continue working with the university. Instead, he chose to follow his own **convictions** and left the university. He found a job working as a **chaplain**, tutoring in the homes of important men in the city. This afforded him time to think and study.

***Book of Common Prayer*:** Prayer book for the Church of England

convictions: Firmly held beliefs

chaplain: Member of the clergy working for an institution or person

John Moves to London

The English Civil War between King Charles I and Parliament broke out in 1642. Owen believed Parliament was right, but the **noblemen** who had hired him sided with the king.

noblemen: Members of the noble or upper class

John felt it was time to move on and went to London where he had some relatives. His rich uncle, unfortunately, stopped supporting him when he discovered John did not support the king. Owen was very discouraged. He had little money, no job, and many questions about his own faith. He often wondered if God even loved him.

John Hears the Gospel

One day Owen was invited by his cousin to go to another town to hear a famous minister preach. His cousin was concerned that lately, John seemed tired and miserably depressed. He thought hearing a stirring sermon might help. Owen felt exhausted and nearly declined the invitation, but he decided to go. For some reason, the preacher they went to hear could not be there, and another minister took his place. This stranger preached a sermon entitled, "Why Are You Fearful, O You of Little Faith?"[83] Owen was **gripped** by this message. As he listened, he realized that

gripped: Deeply affected

through the life, death, and Resurrection of Jesus Christ, God had adopted him — John Owen — as a son. That night, he was assured of his own salvation, and he found new energy and courage.

John spent the next few months writing a book explaining why the Roman Church's teachings were not faithful to Scripture. This was the first of more than 80 books he would write during his lifetime. He was offered a pastorate in the small town of Fordham. This began a more joyful, peaceful time of life. Here, he met and married Mary Rooke.

John Speaks to Parliament

John threw all his newfound energies into teaching and preaching. He was delighted to visit the people of his congregation. He wrote catechisms to clearly explain the Bible's teachings to adults and children. His writings became popular all over England. Owen was a pastor at heart. He was even invited to speak before Parliament in 1646, where he encouraged them to work together with their opponents to solve their differences. These disputes were the cause of the civil war between Charles I and Parliament. At the time Owen spoke to Parliament, King Charles had just surrendered to the Scottish army. He was being held captive until Parliament decided how to handle the situation. Owen strongly spoke against fighting as a means of gaining peace.

On to Coggeshall

Owen was invited to preach to a large congregation in Coggeshall, a town in Essex. Here he was surrounded by a congregation that had been under good preaching. They encouraged him in his work. Sometimes as many as 2,000 people came to hear him preach. As the war slowly approached an end, he preached to the soldiers. He became friends with Lord Fairfax, commander of the Parliamentary army. Owen continued to write extensively, teaching truths from the Bible. He wrote, "When we have communion with God in the doctrine we contend for—then shall we be **garrisoned** by the grace of God against all the assaults of men."[84]

garrisoned: Protected

John Preaches to Parliament Again

King Charles I was tried, convicted, and executed. The English people were shocked. Owen was invited to preach to Parliament once more. To the surprise of his listeners, instead of commenting on what had happened to the king, John urged the lawmakers to allow all groups of Protestant Christians to have the choice to worship freely. His sermon was so well received that in a few months, he was asked again to preach to Parliament. This time, he begged them to make Jesus Christ their Savior and Lord.

Oliver Cromwell, a famous Parliamentary leader, was very impressed by Owen's sermons. He asked Owen to accompany him on his next military expedition to Ireland as chaplain for the troops. Owen did not want to go. He loved his congregation in Coggeshall, but Cromwell would not accept "no" for an answer. Owen diligently preached to the troops and cared for them. He led them in singing the Psalms and studying the Word of God.

While in Ireland, Owen got very sick, so for much of his time there, he stayed in a castle near Dublin, recovering. Before leaving Ireland, he visited Trinity College. He was struck by its lack of teachers and the need for repair. He sensed a real interest in the gospel among the people there, so he spent a great deal of time preaching. When he wasn't

preaching, he worked on another book: *The Death of Death in the Death of Christ*.

After the war with Ireland ended, Owen spoke again to Parliament, begging them to send pastors to Ireland to start churches. That country had been left in ruins. He pleaded, "How is it that Jesus Christ is in Ireland only as a lion staining all His clothes with the blood of His enemies; and there is no one to show that He is a Lamb sprinkled with His own blood for His friends?"[85]

Owen Becomes a Dean at Christ College

Owen was asked to become the dean of Christ College at Oxford. Although he didn't feel qualified to teach theology, he accepted the position. He found the university in bad shape. The Royalist army had been using it for their headquarters during the war. Owen went to work, despite often being sick. He was promoted to **Vice Chancellor** and appointed godly men as professors. This was perhaps the busiest time of his life. Besides teaching and preaching, he did a lot of writing.

> **Vice Chancellor:** Administrator

Interestingly, he dressed like the students instead of wearing the dull clothes and powdered wigs that most professors wore. Some criticized him for it, but he felt he was more approachable to the underclassmen. He identified with his students by wearing bright-colored clothing, velvet coats, high Spanish boots, and a cocked hat. His students admired him and loved listening to his sermons. He **compiled** some of the sermons he preached to students into a book entitled *Mortification of Sin and Overcoming Temptation*. Students today still appreciate his books.

compiled: Assembled

The Great Ejection

When Cromwell retired, Owen returned to Stadhampton where he was born. There he accepted a job as pastor. Oliver Cromwell died in 1658. In 1660, Charles II, son of Charles I, took the throne. He promised the Puritans religious freedom, but within two years, he insisted that all churches follow the *Book of Common Prayer* again. People were no longer free to worship as the Bible taught.

King Charles II set the date of August 24, 1662, as the day when all pastors must make a decision: they were to either abide by his religious rules or be forbidden to ever preach again in his country. When that day arrived, almost 2,000 pastors left England and moved either to other European countries or America. That day became known as the Great Ejection. Throughout his life, Owen had often received many invitations to work and preach in other countries, so he could have accepted one now. He had even been asked to lead a federation of churches and start a university in America. His heart, however, belonged to the English people. He was committed to guiding his countrymen to worship according to the Bible. He sent his wife and children to a safer location at the home of one of Cromwell's former generals.

So many Puritans continued worshiping in England that the king made a new law forbidding more than five people to meet in a home unless they were family members. Then he added more restrictions, stopping any Puritan preacher from going within five miles of any congregation where he had previously preached. This was called the Five Mile Act. Remember, five miles was a long way in those days. Many pastors became very poor and were often hungry. Owen came close to being captured several times. Still, he continued to visit people in their homes, preaching and teaching the Word.

The Plague

In 1665, the Great Plague of London began. It was a terrible illness carried by fleas. It spread all over London. Parliament moved its location, and many rich people fled to their country homes. Most of the doctors even left the city. The king finally ordered the gates to the city shut so no one could leave unless they had a clean bill of health. He was trying to prevent the spread of the disease. Nearly 6,000 people died every week during that summer. About the time that the plague was ending, London had a great fire. In four days and nights, it spread through the city and destroyed most of the buildings. Four-fifths of the city was destroyed. Owen and some other Puritan preachers stayed during the plague to help people. When the fire was over, they ministered to the distraught people. The preachers had some degree of freedom during this time because the authorities were steering clear of the destroyed city.

Owen continued to study and write, instructing people about how to understand God's Word. He had become very well-known and was respected by many people in England. Even the king invited him to discuss issues on several occasions. Each time he met with the king, he begged him to allow religious freedom for the Puritans. He encouraged people to live together in harmony with each other. He even wrote to an important government official, "It seems we are some of the first who ever, anywhere in the world, from the foundation of it, thought of ruining and destroying persons of the same religion with ourselves only because they chose to worship in a different way."[86]

Religious Freedom that Didn't Last

Finally, in 1672, King Charles II declared freedom for Puritans to worship and preach. It was during this time that Owen finally was able to persuade the king to free his friend John Bunyan, who had been imprisoned for years. Bunyan had written *The Pilgrim's Progress* while in jail, and Owen now helped him get his book published. It has become one of the most well-known and loved Christian books in the world.

John Owen's Last Days

Owen's wife, Mary, died in 1676. The couple had lost eleven of their children to disease; only one remained alive. John Owen was 60 years old when Mary died, and he was not in good health himself. A year and a half later, he married Dorothy D'Oyley, who was a great help to him in his old age. She had come from a rich family, and John finally could live comfortably. John struggled with asthma, a condition that made it difficult to breathe at times. John retired in Ealing, a small, quiet village that is now part of London. The day before he died, he wrote his friend, "I am going to Him whom my soul loveth, or rather who has loved me with an everlasting love. I am leaving the ship of the church in a storm; but while the great Pilot is in it, the loss of a poor **under-rower** will be inconsiderable."[87]

under-rower: Servant below deck, slaving away to make the boat go

As John lay dying, he was visited by a friend who brought him good news. His most recent book, *Meditations on the Glory of Christ*, was

ready to go to the publisher. John Owen died on the afternoon of August 24, 1683, exactly 21 years after the Great Ejection.

John Owen's books have been an inspiration throughout the years to countless millions of people. Charles Spurgeon, one of the world's most famous preachers, called John "The Prince of Puritans." His grave bears the inscription, "a traveller on earth who grasped God like one in heaven."[88]

10

John Bunyan

Prisoner for Christ

1628–1688

"*Weep not for me, but for yourselves. I go to the Father of our Lord Jesus Christ, who will, no doubt, through the mediation of His blessed Son, receive me, though a sinner; where I hope we before long shall meet, to sing the new song, and remain everlastingly happy.*"

Elstow, Bedfordshire, England – Bunyan was born in the village of Elstow, just south of Bedford, in 1628.

Bedford, England – Bedford Meeting House was the church where Bunyan preached after joining the Nonconformist movement.

Bedford Gaol (Prison) – He was imprisoned (1660-1672, then again briefly in 1676) for preaching without a license. During his imprisonment, he wrote *The Pilgrim's Progress*.

London, England – Bunyan preached in various churches in London, including those connected to John Owen.

Snow Hill, Holborn, London, England – In 1688, Bunyan died at a friend's house in Snow Hill after falling ill. He was buried alongside other notable figures like John Owen and Isaac Watts.

Who Was John Bunyan?

John Bunyan was a tinker by trade; by the grace of God, he became a preacher. He faced many hardships, dangers, and afflictions in his life. When imprisoned for the sake of the gospel, he wrote the beloved book *The Pilgrim's Progress*. This book showed believers that although life's journey may be hard and cumbersome at times, the Lord will guide them through life and bring them safely to the glorious heavenly home awaiting them.

Early Years

John Bunyan was born in 1628 in the small village of Elstow, near the town of Bedford in England. His father, Thomas, was a tinker, a craftsman who repairs and sells metal utensils. His family was poor, but his father managed to send John to school. John was not taught much about God. He often used bad language and lied. He had many fears as a young boy and into his manhood. He had a couple of close calls with death. Once, he almost drowned; another time, he was nearly bitten by a venomous snake. He sometimes wondered if perhaps he was being punished by God for his sins. He decided that he did not want to think about that anymore.

John Joins the Army

In the summer of 1644, both his mother and sister died. He was very sorrowful because he loved them both dearly. His father quickly remarried. John was 16 years old. He decided to leave home and join the army. Arguments between King Charles I and Parliament had turned into a civil war. Bunyan **enlisted** on the side of Parliament. He often had troubling dreams of hell. Some soldiers thought hell did not exist. Others said God was love; but why, John asked himself, would a God of love have let his mother and sister die? Why did Englishmen keep fighting each other? He tried to force such thoughts from his mind.

enlisted: Joined the army

One day his unit was due to attack a nearby Royalist garrison. John was to serve on sentry duty. That meant he was to stand guard and watch for danger. One of the new soldiers was eager to see some action and begged John to let him do sentry duty in his place. Bunyan agreed and set off to perform **mundane** duties around camp. When the soldiers returned, they seemed strangely quiet and sad. He learned that the eager young boy who had offered to trade duties with him had been killed by an enemy musket ball.

mundane: Dull or ordinary

That should have hit him — Bunyan trembled at the thought of it. A fellow soldier said, "All I can say is God must have plans for you, Bunyan. Although I have no idea why He'd want to use such a foul-mouthed rascal."[89] Bunyan felt it must be another warning from God.

Home from the War

In July 1647, Parliament **disbanded** the **regiment** to which Bunyan was assigned, and he returned home to join his father as a tinker. He traveled around the countryside, fixing pots, pans, and metal tools at homes and farms. He soon met a poor but upright young woman and asked her to marry him. She owned two Puritan books that her father had given her. Sometimes, she requested John to read them to her. He and his family started attending church faithfully and following some of the advice he read about in the books. He became convicted about his bad language and stopped that nasty habit. People in town were impressed that he was cleaning up his life, but he knew his heart had not changed. One day, he stopped to listen to two women talking about God. They were discussing how no one could go to heaven just because they had done

disbanded: Dissolved

regiment: Unit in the army

good things. They spoke joyfully about the Bible and their church. They introduced him to their pastor, John Gifford.

This church in Bedford was congregational in nature, meaning the congregation made decisions instead of having to ask bishops or kings for permission or rulings. Gifford preached the gospel clearly. He and Bunyan had similar upbringings; Gifford had been rebellious as a youth. He invited Bunyan into his home and taught him how to understand the Bible. John was given a copy of a book by Martin Luther explaining Paul's letter to the Galatians. It was old and falling apart, but next to the Bible, this became Bunyan's favorite book.

John Bunyan Is Saved

One day while walking through a field, John seemed to feel the heaviness of his many sins like a burden weighing him down. He was convinced that his own righteousness could never be enough. Suddenly, this thought came to him: "Thy righteousness is in heaven."[90] He realized that Jesus Christ had taken the punishment for his sins on the Cross and given John Bunyan the gift of His righteousness. Bunyan went home with a happy heart.

He continued to grow in the faith under the guidance of Pastor Gifford. John could not get enough of the Bible, and he could not help but share the good news of the gospel with people he met.

John Bunyan the Preacher

Although John was never officially ordained, Pastor Gifford gave him opportunities to preach. People were excited about his messages. He had a gift for teaching the Bible in ways people could understand. His personal application and illustrations made the Bible come alive for his listeners. "Amazement of God's grace in saving such a great sinner created within him what he called 'a fire in mine own conscience.' "[91]

In 1658, John's wife died, leaving him with four children to care for. To make matters worse, his oldest daughter, Mary, was blind. Around that time, King Charles II, son of Charles I, was influenced to take back the English throne. This caused trouble for Puritan preachers.

Bunyan Is Jailed

In November 1660, Bunyan was asked to preach at a small farm ten miles south of Bedford. When local authorities heard of it, they decided to stop the meeting. A friend warned Bunyan, but he thought fleeing would set a bad example. Just as he was getting ready to preach, he was arrested. He was taken to the justice of the peace, Sir Francis Wingate, in the town of Dunstable. Wingate found him guilty of not attending the Church of England and of meeting with other Christians to preach. He told John that if he agreed to stop preaching, he could go free. Bunyan, however, could not do this in good conscience. He was sent to jail for three months and warned that if he did not return to the Church of England at the end of that time, he would be **banned** from England. If he ever came back to England, he would be killed.

By this time, Bunyan had remarried. He knew he was responsible for providing for his wife, Elizabeth; his four children; and the new baby Elizabeth

banned: Driven out

was expecting. He wrote a letter asking for a new trial. His wife delivered it to the judges in person. Although they did not allow him another trial, the jailer had pity on Bunyan and allowed him to go home for short periods of time. He was able to travel to London and preach while there. John's enemies found out and threatened to take the jailer to court, so after that, he was not allowed any days of freedom. The authorities offered him freedom only if he agreed to stop preaching. Bunyan said, "I have determined, the Almighty God being my help and shield, yet to suffer, if frail life might continue so long, even till the moss shall grow on mine eyebrows, rather than thus violate my faith and principles."[92]

Bunyan used his jail time to write books and preach to fellow inmates. He also learned to make shoelaces to sell, which helped to provide income for his family. Having other Christians as fellow prisoners made Bunyan's time easier. They discussed the Scriptures together and took turns preaching on Sundays. They talked about how to better organize local preachers.

Bunyan Is Released

In 1672, the law changed, and Bunyan was released and permitted to preach. Four years later, however, he was sent back to jail. As usual, he spent his time writing and preaching.

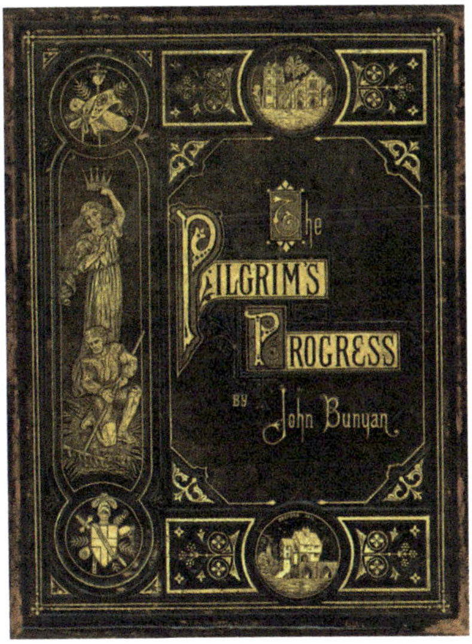

Pilgrim's Progress, Master Books

During his lifetime, he wrote 60 books. *The Pilgrim's Progress* was the most popular. This book is the story of a man named Christian, who wrestles with his sin until his burden is lifted at the Cross of Calvary. He faces many troubles and struggles along the way until he finally reaches heaven. Some people think Bunyan based the book on his own life and the afflictions he faced.

Declaration of Indulgences

In March 1672, King Charles II released a **Declaration of Indulgences**, which repealed the previous laws against Puritan pastors. Bunyan was finally released after 12 years of imprisonment. In 1673, the Church of England became concerned about the number of Puritan preachers and forced Charles to revoke the declaration. Bunyan was imprisoned a second time and released in six months. John Owen helped to get Bunyan liberated from jail. Owen also got his publisher to print *The Pilgrim's Progress*. Next to the Bible, *The Pilgrim's Progress* became the second most popular book ever. When the pastor of the church in Bedford died, the congregation called Bunyan, even though he was still in prison. He remained their pastor until his death. Owen thought so much of Bunyan's preaching that he invited him a few times to preach at his church. Owen commented that "he would gladly exchange all his learning for Bunyan's ability to preach the gospel to the common people."[93]

Declaration of Indulgences: A proclamation

Bunyan's Last Days

For the next few years, Bunyan preached in many villages and towns, and even in London. He spoke to crowds that numbered from 1,000 to 3,000 people. He continued to write and produced a **sequel** to *The Pilgrim's Progress*, as well as numerous other titles. Sometimes, he narrowly escaped arrest. During the summer of 1688, a neighbor implored Bunyan to ride 40 miles to counsel a father and son who needed help resolving a conflict. He was successful in his mission but was caught in a thunderstorm on the way back. He stopped at the house of a friend who lived in London. He began to feel sick but still managed to preach at Whitechapel on Sunday, August 19. He preached about Christian's escape from the dungeon of sin and his final entry to the Celestial City. This was from his book *The Pilgrim's Progress*. He grew feverish, and by the time he got home, he felt worse. It soon became obvious that he was dying. Friends came to see him one last time. He told them, "Weep not for me, but for yourselves. I go to the Father of our Lord Jesus Christ, who will, no doubt, through the mediation of His blessed Son, receive me, though a sinner; where I hope we before long shall meet, to sing the new song, and remain everlastingly happy, world without end. My greatest desire is to be with Christ."[94] He lifted his hands toward heaven and cried, "Take me, for I come to Thee."[95] With that exclamation, he died.

sequel: Another book in the series

John Bunyan was buried in Bunhill Fields in London. *The Pilgrim's Progress* has since been translated into over 200 languages. Within a year after John Bunyan died, William and Mary came into power in England and established a constitutional monarchy, which limited the power of rulers and granted religious freedom to all people. The fight for religious liberty that John Bunyan had championed for so many years was now over.

Timeline

A.D. 1 –100	33	Death and Resurrection of Jesus
	34	Conversion of Saul of Tarsus
	42	Persecution in Palestine under Herod Agrippa
	64	Persecution in Rome under Nero
	64 or 67	Peter is martyred
	69	Birth of Polycarp
	95	Persecution under Domitian
	96	Revelation of John on island of Patmos
	100	Death of Apostle John in Ephesus
101 –200	107	Ignatius is martyred in Rome
	130	Irenaeus is born
	154	Polycarp visits bishop of Rome, possibly with Irenaeus

101–200	155	Polycarp is martyred in Smyrna by Roman government
	177	Irenaeus is in France and becomes the bishop of Lyons
	182–188	Irenaeus writes *Against Heresies*

201–500	202	Persecution under Emperor Septimus Severus
	202	Irenaeus dies
	ca. 387	Patrick is born in Bannaventa Taburniae, in Britain
	ca. 405	Patrick is kidnapped and taken as a slave to Ireland
	ca. 411	Patrick escapes and returns home
	ca.450	Patrick goes to Ireland as a missionary
	ca. 461	Patrick dies in Ireland

1301–1400	1324	John Wycliffe is born in Yorkshire, England
	1340	Wycliffe enters Oxford University
	1348	The Black Death comes to England

1301–1400	1356	John Wycliffe receives his B.A. degree
	1358	Wycliffe receives M.A. degree
	1361	Wycliffe appointed bishop in Fillingham, Lincolnshire, England
	1372	Wycliffe awarded doctor of divinity degree
	1382	Bible translated into English
	1384	Wycliffe dies
1401–1500	1427	Wycliffe's bones dug up, burned, and scattered
	1454	Gutenberg Bible printed
	1483	Birth of Martin Luther in Germany
	1492	Columbus discovers America
	1494	William Tyndale is born
	1497	Luther goes to school in Magdeburg, about the same time as Columbus' third trip to America

1501 –1600

1501	Luther goes to school in Erfurt
1507	Luther is ordained a priest
1508	Luther teaches theology at Wittenberg
1509	Henry VIII becomes king
1509	John Calvin is born
1512	William Tyndale receives his B.A. at Oxford
1513	Battle of Flodden
1514	John Knox is born in Haddington, Scotland
1515	Tyndale receives his M.A at Oxford
1517	Luther nails his *95 Theses* to the door of Castle Church in Wittenberg
1519	Luther's *95 Theses* have been translated into French, English, and Latin
1521	Diet of Worms
1521	Tyndale joins the house of Sir John Walsh

1501 – 1600

1521	Henry VIII is made Defender of the Faith by Pope Leo X
1521	Luther takes refuge in Wartburg Castle
1522	Luther translates the New Testament into German
1522	Tyndale is summoned to the diocese on charge of heresy
1523	Tyndale leaves for London
1524	Tyndale arrives in Hamburg, Germany
1524	Tyndale visits Wittenberg
1525	Luther marries Katherine von Bora
1526	Luther's first son is born
1526	English New Testaments arrive in England
1527	Luther's first daughter is born
1528	Luther's first daughter dies
1528	John Calvin goes to study law and is converted

1501–1600

1528	Patrick Hamilton is the first Scot to be killed for his faith
1529	Luther's second daughter is born
1529	Protestants acquire their name
1531	Luther's second son is born
1533	Luther's third son is born
1533	Henry VIII marries Anne Boleyn
1534	Luther's youngest daughter is born
1534	Old and New Testaments now published in German
1535	Tyndale arrested in Antwerp
1536	Tyndale is condemned as a heretic and put to death
1536	Anne Boleyn is put to death
1536	Henry VIII marries Jane Seymour
1536	Wales and England become one kingdom

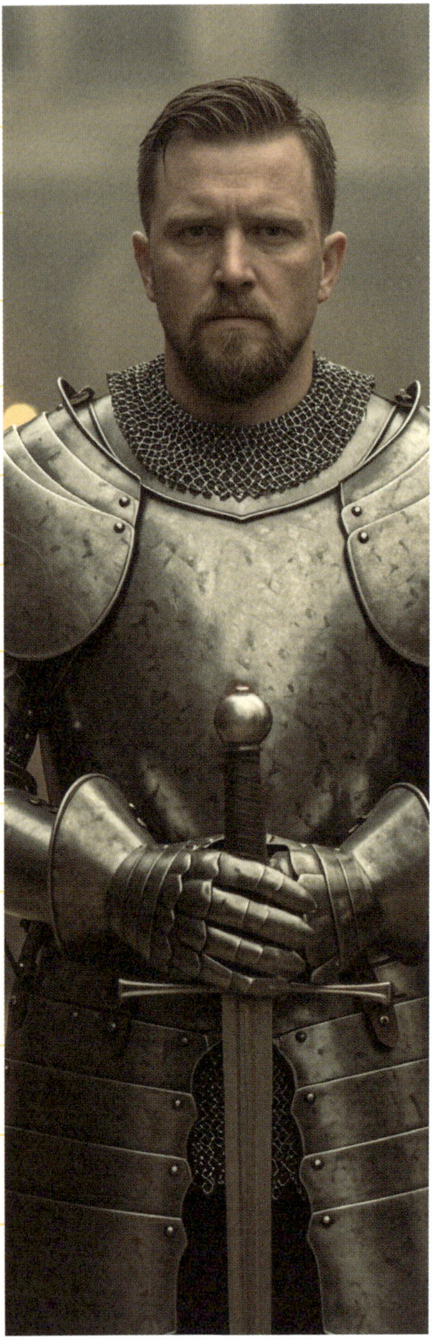

1501 –1600

1536	First publication of John Calvin's *Institutes of the Christian Religion*
1536	Calvin sets off for Strasbourg but is persuaded to remain in Geneva
1537	Jane Seymour dies after giving birth to Edward VI, heir to the throne
1538	Calvin banished from Geneva
1539	Every church in England receives a copy of the English Bible
1539	Calvin becomes a citizen of Strasbourg
1540	John Calvin marries Idelette de Bure
1540	Calvin publishes commentary on Romans
1541	Calvin returns to Geneva
1542	Luther's second daughter dies at age 13
1542	John Calvin's son dies

1501 –1600

1542	King James V dies; baby Mary Stuart becomes queen
1545	Knox follows George Wishart
1546	Luther dies
1546–1548	John Calvin publishes commentaries on 1 Corinthians, 2 Corinthians, Galatians, Ephesians, Philippians, Colossians, 1 Timothy, 2 Timothy.
1547	Knox moves into the castle at St. Andrews
1547	Knox preaches his first sermon
1547	Knox is taken to be a galley slave for 19 months
1549	John Calvin's wife dies
1549	John Knox becomes a pastor in Berwick, England
1550–1551	John Calvin publishes commentaries on Thessalonians, James, 1 and 2 Peter, Jude

1501 –1600

1550	Knox meets Margery Bowes, who will become his wife
1552	Knox moves to London to become one of the king's preachers
1553	John Calvin publishes commentaries on Acts, Isaiah, Gospel of John
1553	Knox is forced to hide again when Mary Tudor becomes queen
1554	John Knox flees to France, then Zurich, and then Geneva, Switzerland
1554	John Knox pastors a small English church in Frankfurt, Germany
1555	Knox goes back to Geneva; he returns to Scotland and marries Margery Bowes
1556	Knox returns to Geneva with his wife and mother-in-law

1501 –1600

1558	Elizabeth I becomes queen of England
1559	Final edition of John Calvin's *Institutes of the Christian Religion* is published
1559	Knox returns to Scotland
1559	Geneva Academy opens
1559	Calvin becomes citizen of Geneva
1560	Geneva Bible published
1560	Mary of Guise dies
1560	Knox becomes pastor in Edinburgh; Margery dies
1561	Mary Stuart returns to Scotland
1564	Calvin publishes commentary on Joshua
1564	John Calvin dies
1564	Knox marries Margaret Stewart
1567	Mary Stuart is forced to give up her crown
1572	Knox dies of pneumonia

1601 –1700

1616	John Owen is born
1628	Owen enters college
1628	John Bunyan is born in Elstow, England
1635	Owen receives his master’s degree
1637	Owen leaves Oxford University
1642	English Civil War begins
1642	Owen hears a sermon that leads to his salvation
1642	Owen writes his first book
1643	Owen pastors in Fordham
1643	Owen gets married to Mary Rooke
1644	John Bunyan joins Parliamentary army during First English Civil War
1646	Owen preaches before Parliament
1647	Bunyan returns home
1649	King Charles is executed

1601 – 1700

1649	Oliver Cromwell takes Owen to Ireland as chaplain
1650	Bunyan goes to church and gets saved
1651	Owen teaches at Oxford University
1655	Bunyan begins to preach
1658	Cromwell dies
1659	Bunyan's first wife dies, leaving him with four children
1659	Bunyan marries second wife, Elizabeth
1660	Owen leaves Oxford
1660	Charles II returns from exile to become king again
1660	Bunyan is arrested for preaching
1661	Bunyan is jailed
1662	Puritan pastors forbidden to preach
1665	The Great Plague spreads in London

1601 – 1700

1666	The Great Fire of London occurs
1666	Bunyan writes an account of his life
1671	Bunyan is appointed pastor to his church at Bedford
1672	King gives temporary freedom to Puritans
1672	Bunyan is released from prison
1675	Owen's wife, Mary, dies
1677	Bunyan is arrested again and imprisoned for six months
1678	Bunyan publishes *The Pilgrim's Progress*
1683	John Owen dies
1684	Bunyan publishes *The Pilgrim's Progress: Part 2*
1687	James II issues new Declaration of Indulgence
1688	Bunyan dies with fever
1689	The Act of Toleration gives Puritans the right to worship legally

Corresponding Curriculum

Legends of the Faith Series
Early Church Fathers • Book 1

All the stories in this book can correspond with the following Master Books Curriculum:

- *The World's Story 1: The Ancients*
- *The World's Story 1 Timeline: The Ancients (Timeline Pack)*
- *The World's Story 2: Middle Ages*
- *The World's Story 2: Middle Ages (Timeline Pack)*
- *Map Trek: Set (Atlas and Outlines)*
- *Wonders of Old: A Blank Timeline Book of World History*
- *Big Book of History*
- *Elementary World History: You Report*
- *Language Lessons for a Living Education*
- *Elementary Geography and Cultures*
- *A Child's Geography Vol. 2: Explore the Holy Land*
- *A Child's Geography Vol. 4: Explore Medieval Kingdoms*
- *The Annals of the World*
- *Adams' Chart of History*
- *Children's Atlas of God's World*

Glossary

Abyss: Pit.

Ascended: To rise up through the air.

Banished: Gotten rid of.

Banned: Driven out.

Bishop: An elder in charge of a local church or churches.

Blaspheme: Deny.

***Book of Common Prayer*:** Prayer book for the Church of England.

Catalyst: Spark.

Centurion: Roman commander.

Chaplain: Member of the clergy working for an institution or person.

Collapsed: Fell.

Commissioned: Set apart for special service.

Compiled: Assembled.

Conversion: When one becomes a Christian.

Converted: Embraced the gospel.

Convictions: Firmly held beliefs.

Corruption: Dishonest conduct.

Debts: Money owed to others.

Declaration of Indulgences: A proclamation.

Devastation: Damage.

Devout: Deeply committed.

Diaconum: Deacon.

Disbanded: Dissolved.

Disguised: Hid his identity.

Distraught: Very upset.

Duchess of Ferrara: An Italian noblewoman.

Enlisted: Joined the army.

Ephesus: A large city in Asia Minor.

Epitaph: Words written in memory of a person.

Era: A period of history.

Excommunicate: Officially exclude from the Church.

Exiled: Forced to leave his country.

Fugitive: One who lives in hiding.

Friars: Men devoted to religious groups within the Roman Church.

Garrisoned: Protected.

Gentiles: People who are not Jewish.

Gnostics: A group that believed in secret knowledge.

"Gods": Statues, images, or even ideas worshiped instead of the One true God.

Gripped: Deeply affected.

Heretic: One whose beliefs oppose what the Church teaches.

Indulgences: Pieces of parchment sold to people as payment for their sins.

Inherited: Born with.

Justified: Right.

Keen: Strong.

Kidnapped: Taken away by force.

Kindled: Started.

Knights: Soldiers.

Lay: Common.

Lutheranism: Branch of Protestant Christianity based on Martin Luther's teaching.

Luxuries: Extravagant living.

Martyr: One who dies for the sake of the gospel.

Monk: A man who lives a secluded life in a monastery to spend time in prayer and meditation.

Mundane: Dull or ordinary.

***Ninety-five Theses*:** Points or ideas.

Noblemen: Members of the noble or upper class.

Pagan: Ungodly.

Pentateuch: First five books of the Bible.

Persecution: Ill-treatment.

Piqued: Excited or stirred.

Pneumonia: Painful lung infection that makes it hard to breathe.

Pope: Head of the Roman Church.

Prior: One in authority of a religious house.

Proconsul: Governor of a province in ancient Rome.

Providentially: Divine intervention by God.

Raiders: Persons who attack and steal.

Reconciled: Restored.

Reformation: A period when the Church underwent a revival and returned to original doctrines found in the Scripture.

Refuge: Safe place.

Refute: Prove wrong.

Regent: A person who governs a kingdom for a ruler who is a child.

Regiment: Unit in the army.

Renounce: Formally abandon.

Repenting: Asking forgiveness for.

Retract: Take back.

Rituals: Practices or ceremonies.

Rubbish: Garbage.

Saint: Someone especially close to God.

Seized: Taken by force.

Sequel: Another book in the series.

Subdued: Softened.

Summoned: Called.

Supervisor: Leader of employees.

Tedious: Long and difficult.

Theology: The study of God.

Treason: Disloyalty to one's country.

Tutor: A person hired to teach children.

Uncivilized: Considered wild and uneducated.

Under-rower: Servant below deck, slaving away to make the boat go.

Urgency: Strong need.

Vice Chancellor: Administrator.

Endnotes

1. Simonetta Carr, *Church History* (Grand Rapids, MI: Reformation Heritage Books, 2022), 8.
2. Sinclair. B. Ferguson, *Polycarp of Smyrna: The Man Whose Faith Lasted* (Carlisle, PA: The Banner of Truth Trust, 2010), 12.
3. Ibid., 18.
4. William Chad Newsom, *Polycarp: The Crown of Fire* (Scotland, UK: Christian Focus, 2005), 169.
5. Ferguson, *Polycarp of Smyrna*, 32.
6. Simonetta Carr, *Irenaeus of Lyon* (Grand Rapids, MI: Reformation Heritage Books, 2017), 8.
7. Newsom, *Polycarp*, 186.
8. Sinclair Ferguson, *Irenaeus of Lyon* (Carlisle, PA: The Banner of Truth Trust, 2020), 35.
9. Ibid., 31.
10. Carr, *Church History*, 10.
11. Carr, *Irenaeus of Lyon*, 51.
12. Ibid., 51.
13. Simonetta Carr, *Patrick of Ireland* (Grand Rapids, MI: Reformation Heritage Books, 2023) 8.
14. K.C. Murdarasi, *Patrick of Ireland: The Boy Who Forgave* (Scotland, UK: Christian Focus Publications, 2015), 11.
15. Carr, *Patrick of Ireland*, 16.
16. Ibid., 16.
17. Ibid., 18.
18. Murdarasi, *Patrick of Ireland*, 41.
19. Carr, *Patrick of Ireland*, 28.
20. Murdarasi, *Patrick of Ireland*, 50.
21. Carr, *Patrick of Ireland*, 35.
22. Ibid., 41.
23. Murdarasi, *Patrick of Ireland*, 106.
24. Ibid., 108.
25. Diana Kleyn and Joel Beeke, *Reformation Heroes* (Grand Rapids, MI: Reformation Heritage Books, 2007), 7.
26. David Luckman, *John Wycliffe: According to the Word* (Scotland, UK: Christian Focus Publications, 2024), 14.
27. Ibid., 20. Emphasis added.
28. Ibid., 26.
29. Steven Lawson, *The Bible Convictions of John Wycliffe* (Sanford, FL: Ligonier Ministries, 2021), 44.
30. Luckman, *John Wycliffe*, 76.
31. Kleyn and Beeke, *Reformation Heroes*, 11.
32. Lawson, *The Bible Convictions of John Wycliffe*, 158.
33. Kleyn and Beeke, *Reformation Heroes*, 15.
34. Luckman, *John Wycliffe*, 99.
35. Ibid., 123.
36. Simonetta Carr, *Martin Luther* (Grand Rapids, MI: Reformation Heritage Books, 2016), 18.
37. Diana Kleyn and Joel Beeke, *Reformation Heroes* (Grand Rapids, MI: Reformation Heritage Books, 2007), 30.
38. Catherine Mackenzie, *Martin Luther: Reformation Fire* (Scotland, UK: Christian Focus Publications, 2016), 97.
39. Paul L. Maier, *Martin Luther: The Man Who Changed the World* (St. Louis, MO: Concordia Publishing Company, 2004,) 12.
40. Mackenzie, *Martin Luther*, 107.
41. Carr, *Martin Luther*, 37.
42. Ibid., 52.
43. Ibid., 54.
44. Diana Kleyn and Joel Beeke, *Reformation Heroes* (Grand Rapids, MI: Reformation Heritage Books, 2007), 64.
45. Ibid., 64.
46. William Tyndale, "The Preface of Master Tyndale, That He Made Before the Five Books of Moses, Called Genesis," in *The Works of William Tyndale*, 1848/rept. (Edinburgh, Scotland: The Banner of Truth, 2010), 394. Emphasis added.

47. Kleyn and Beeke, *Reformation Heroes*, 68.
48. Ibid.
49. Ibid.
50. Ibid., 69.
51. Ibid., 70.
52. Ibid., 71.
53. Lori Rich, *William Tyndale: Bible Smuggler* (Scotland, UK: Christian Focus, 2004), 137.
54. Ibid., 137.
55. Diana Kleyn and Joel Beeke, *Reformation Heroes* (Grand Rapids, MI: Reformation Heritage Books, 2007), 119. Emphases added.
56. Simonetta Carr, *John Calvin* (Grand Rapids, MI: Reformation Heritage Books, 2008), 23.
57. Kleyn and Beeke, *Reformation Heroes*, 123.
58. Ibid., 123.
59. W. Robert Godfrey, *John Calvin: Pilgrim and Pastor* (Wheaton, IL: Crossway Books, 2009), 31–32.
60. Carr, *John Calvin*, 35.
61. Ibid., 125.
62. Ibid., 40.
63. Kleyn and Beeke, *Reformation Heroes*, 125.
64. Carr, *John Calvin*, 45.
65. Ibid., 47.
66. Godfrey, *John Calvin*, 195.
67. Carr, *John Calvin*, 55.
68. Ibid., 56.
69. Godfrey, *John Calvin*, 199.
70. Carr, *John Calvin*, 58.
71. Godfrey, *John Calvin*, 199.
72. Simonetta Carr, *John Knox* (Grand Rapids, MI: Reformation Heritage Books, 2014), 8.
73. Diana Kleyn and Joel Beeke, *Reformation Heroes* (Grand Rapids, MI: Reformation Heritage Books, 2007), 93.
74. Ibid., 95.
75. Carr, *John Knox*, 27.
76. Ibid., 30.
77. Ibid., 37.
78. Kleyn and Beeke, *Reformation Heroes*, 97.
79. Ibid.
80. Carr, *John Knox*, 52.
81. Kleyn and Beeke, *Reformation Heroes*, 99.
82. Ibid.
83. Simonetta Carr, *John Owen* (Grand Rapids, MI: Reformation Heritage Books, 2010), 14.
84. Glenda Faye Mathes and Joel R. Beeke, *Puritan Heroes* (Grand Rapids, MI: Reformation Heritage Books, 2018), 110. Emphasis added.
85. Ibid., 111.
86. Carr, *John Owen*, 48.
87. Ibid., 52. Emphasis added.
88. Ibid., 54.
89. Glenda Faye Mathes and Joel R. Beeke, *Puritan Heroes* (Grand Rapids, MI: Reformation Heritage Books, 2018), 128.
90. Simonetta Carr, *John Bunyan* (Grand Rapids, MI: Reformation Heritage Books, 2020), 20.
91. Mathes and Beeke, *Puritan Heroes*, 131.
92. Ibid., 137.
93. Carr, *John Bunyan*, 45.
94. Mathes and Beeke, *Puritan Heroes*, 138.
95. Ibid., 138.